Unit Resource Guide
Unit 6

More Adding and Subtracting

THIRD EDITION

KENDALL/HUNT PUBLISHING COMPANY
4050 Westmark Drive   Dubuque, Iowa 52002

A TIMS® Curriculum
University of Illinois at Chicago

UIC The University of Illinois
at Chicago

The original edition was based on work supported by the National Science Foundation under grant No. MDR 9050226 and the University of Illinois at Chicago. Any opinions, findings, and conclusions or recommendations expressed in this publication are those of the author(s) and do not necessarily reflect the views of the granting agencies.

Letter Home

More Adding and Subtracting

Date: _____

Dear Family Member:

In this unit, we continue the study of addition and subtraction concepts by introducing formal methods for adding and subtracting numbers up to four digits (through the thousands). We begin by representing problems using base-ten pieces and then introduce written procedures. Your child will have numerous opportunities to refine his or her skills with addition and subtraction.

Although we focus on one paper-and-pencil procedure for adding and subtracting, keep in mind that other methods work just as well. For example, the procedures taught in other countries often differ from the standard ones taught here. Encourage your child to use an appropriate method that makes sense to him or her.

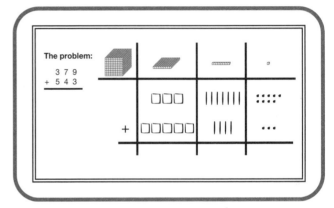

A second focus of the unit is to develop skills that help students estimate the answer to a problem. It is not always necessary to find an exact answer, but it is often critical to know when an answer is reasonable.

Students use base-ten pieces to solve addition problems.

You can provide additional support at home in the following ways.

- **Practice Estimating Sums.** Encourage your child to estimate your grocery bill.
- **Books.** Three books that complement this unit are *The 500 Hats of Bartholomew Cubbins* by Dr. Seuss, *Henry Huggins* by Beverly Cleary, and *A Million Fish . . . More or Less* by Patricia McKissack.
- **Digits Game.** Play the *Digits Game* with your child.
- **Math Facts.** Continue to help your child practice all the subtraction facts using the *Subtraction Flash Cards.*

Sincerely,

_____

Carta al hogar

Más sumas y restas

Fecha: _____

Estimado miembro de familia:

En esta unidad, seguiremos estudiando los conceptos de la suma y de la resta presentando métodos formales para sumar y restar números de hasta cuatro dígitos (hasta las unidades de mil). Comenzaremos representando problemas usando piezas de base diez y luego presentaremos los procedimientos escritos. Su hijo/a tendrá numerosas oportunidades para afinar sus habilidades de suma y resta.

Aunque pondremos énfasis en un procedimiento de papel y lápiz específico, recuerde que otros métodos también pueden funcionar. Por ejemplo, los procedimientos que se enseñan en otros países a menudo difieren de los procedimientos comunes que se enseñan aquí. Anime a su hijo/a a usar un método apropiado que tenga sentido para él o ella.

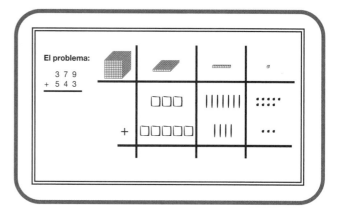

Un segundo enfoque de esta unidad es desarrollar habilidades para ayudar a los estudiantes a estimar la respuesta a un problema. No siempre es necesario encontrar la respuesta exacta, pero algunas veces es importante saber que la respuesta es razonable.

Los estudiantes usan piezas de base diez para resolver problemas de suma.

Usted puede ayudar a su hijo/a en casa de las siguientes maneras:

- **Practicar estimaciones de sumas.** Anime a su hijo/a a estimar el total de la cuenta cuando vayan de compras al supermercado.
- **Libros.** Los tres libros que complementan esta unidad son, *500 Hats of Bartholomew Cubbins* de Dr. Seuss. *Henry Huggins* de Beverly Clearly, y *A Million Fish . . . More or Less* de Patricia McKissack.
- **Juego con dígitos.** Juegue al *Juego con dígitos* con su hijo/a.
- **Conceptos básicos.** Siga ayudando a su hijo/a a practicar todas las restas básicas usando las tarjetas de resta.

Atentamente,

_____

Table of Contents

Unit 6
More Adding and Subtracting

Unit 6

Outline
More Adding and Subtracting

Estimated Class Sessions

16-18

Unit Summary

Students' experiences with two-digit addition and subtraction, base-ten pieces, and a standard algorithm are extended to three- and four-digit numbers. Students continue developing their own strategies for adding and subtracting large numbers and they learn to use standard procedures. The emphasis is on solving problems involving addition and subtraction in context. The Adventure Book *Leonardo the Blockhead* looks at the historical and multicultural roots of the base-ten number system we use today. The DPP for this unit develops strategies for the multiplication facts for the nines.

Major Concept Focus

- number sense
- partitioning
- place value
- ordering large numbers
- base-ten system
- multidigit addition
- multidigit subtraction
- addition algorithms
- subtraction algorithms
- computational estimation
- rounding
- *Adventure Book:* addition and subtraction algorithms
- Game: multidigit addition and subtraction
- Student Rubric: *Knowing*
- palindromes
- communicating problem solving
- multiplication strategies for the 9s

Pacing Suggestions

This unit develops concepts, estimation, and paper-and-pencil skills for addition and subtraction. Use the recommended session numbers for each lesson as a guide. It is not necessary to stay on a topic until students master each skill, especially paper-and-pencil procedures, as students will revisit them in later units. Practice is distributed throughout the year in the Daily Practice and Problems and Home Practice.

Assessment Indicators

Use the following Assessment Indicators and the *Observational Assessment Record* that follows the Background section in this unit to assess students on key ideas.

A1. Can students represent addition and subtraction using base-ten pieces?

A2. Can students add multidigit numbers using paper and pencil?

A3. Can students subtract multidigit numbers using paper and pencil?

A4. Can students estimate sums and differences?

A5. Can students determine the reasonableness of a solution?

A6. Can students solve problems involving addition and subtraction?

Unit Planner

	Lesson Information	Supplies	Copies/Transparencies
Lesson 1 **The 500 Hats** URG Pages 27–32 DPP A–B HP Part 1 *Estimated Class Sessions* **1**	**Activity** *The 500 Hats of Bartholomew Cubbins* provides a context for partitioning, adding, and subtracting two- and three-digit numbers. **Math Facts** DPP Task B provides practice with multiplication facts for the nines. **Homework** 1. Students can write other stories with addition and subtraction problems. 2. Assign Part 1 of the Home Practice. **Assessment** Use the *Observational Assessment Record* to note students' abilities to solve problems involving addition and subtraction using mental strategies.	• 1 set of base-ten pieces (2 packs, 14 flats, 30 skinnies, and 50 bits) per student pair or group of three • 1 calculator per student, optional • *The 500 Hats of Bartholomew Cubbins* by Dr. Seuss or another story that refers to numbers in the hundreds	• 1 copy of *Observational Assessment Record* URG Pages 13–14 to be used throughout this unit
Lesson 2 **The Coat of Many Bits** URG Pages 33–40 SG Page 66 DPP C–F *Estimated Class Sessions* **2-3**	**Activity** Students trace an outline of their coats or jackets onto a sheet of paper and measure the area covered by the outline. The data collected is used in several problem situations. **Math Facts** DPP items C, D, and F provide practice with math facts. **Homework** Students complete *Questions 5–7* on *The Coat of Many Bits* Activity Page.	• 1 student's coat (or jacket, sweater, or sweatshirt) per student group • 1 large sheet of paper at least 2 yards by 1 yard per student group • 1 set of base-ten pieces (14 flats, 30 skinnies, and 50 bits) per student pair or group of three • crayons • 1 index card per student group • tape • 1 pair of scissors per student group	
Lesson 3 **Adding with Base-Ten Pieces** URG Pages 41–60 SG Pages 67–70 DAB Pages 103–104 DPP G–L HP Part 2	**Activity** Students expand their understanding of addition and place value with larger numbers. **Math Facts** DPP Challenge H provides practice with multiplication facts. **Homework** 1. Assign *Questions 3–6* on the *Adding on the Base-Ten Board* Activity Pages in the *Discovery Assignment Book* after Part 1. 2. Assign the Homework section in the *Student Guide* after Part 2.	• 1 set of base-ten pieces (2 packs, 14 flats, 30 skinnies, and 50 bits) per student pair or group of three	• 1 copy of *Base-Ten Board* URG Pages 51–52 per student pair • 1 copy of *Base-Ten Recording Sheet* URG Page 53 per student • 1 transparency of *Base-Ten Board* URG Pages 51–52, optional • 1 transparency of *Base-Ten Recording Sheet* URG Page 53, optional

	Lesson Information	Supplies	Copies/Transparencies
Estimated Class Sessions **3-4**	3. Assign Part 2 of the Home Practice for more practice with addition and subtraction. **Assessment** Use the *Observational Assessment Record* to note students' progress representing addition using base-ten pieces.		
Lesson 4 **Subtracting with Base-Ten Pieces** URG Pages 61–79 SG Pages 71–76 DAB Pages 105–108 DPP M–T **Estimated Class Sessions** **4**	**Activity** Students expand their understanding of subtraction and place value with larger numbers. **Homework** 1. Assign the Homework section of the *Subtracting on the Base-Ten Board* Activity Pages in the *Discovery Assignment Book* after Part 1. 2. Assign the Homework section in the *Student Guide* after Part 2. **Assessment** 1. Use **Questions 6–14** in the *Student Guide* to assess students' abilities to solve problems involving addition and subtraction. **Question 10** can be scored using the Knowing dimension of the *TIMS Multidimensional Rubric*. 2. Use the Homework section in the *Discovery Assignment Book* and the *Observational Assessment Record* to note students' progress subtracting using base-ten pieces and paper and pencil. 3. Use Task R as a short assessment.	• 1 set of base-ten pieces (2 packs, 14 flats, 30 skinnies, and 50 bits) per student pair or group of three	• 1 copy of *Base-Ten Board* URG Pages 51–52 per student pair • 1 copy of *Base-Ten Recording Sheet* URG Page 53 per student • 1 transparency of *Base-Ten Board* URG Pages 51–52, optional • 1 transparency of *Base-Ten Recording Sheet* URG Page 53, optional • 1 copy of *TIMS Multidimensional Rubric* TIG, Assessment section
Lesson 5 **Close Enough!** URG Pages 80–90 SG Pages 77–80 DPP U–Z **Estimated Class Sessions** **3**	**Activity** Students explore estimation strategies and round to the nearest ten and hundred. **Math Facts** DPP Task V provides practice with math facts. **Homework** Assign the Homework section in the *Student Guide.* **Assessment** Use the *Observational Assessment Record* to note students' abilities to estimate sums and differences using convenient numbers.	• 1 set of base-ten pieces (14 flats, 30 skinnies, and 50 bits) per student pair or group of three and 1 set for the teacher	• 2 copies of *Hundreds Template* URG Page 88 per student pair or more as needed • 2 transparencies of *Hundreds Template* URG Page 88 or more as needed

(Continued)

	Lesson Information	Supplies	Copies/Transparencies
Lesson 6 **Leonardo the Blockhead** URG Pages 91–100 AB Pages 43–58 DPP AA–BB *Estimated Class Sessions* **1**	**Adventure Book** This story is based upon the role of the great Italian mathematician Fibonacci in the introduction of the Hindu-Arabic numeration and associated algorithms into Europe. **Assessment** Use DPP Bit AA as an assessment of students' progress with subtraction.	• map of Europe, North Africa, and the Middle East, optional	
Lesson 7 **Palindromes** URG Pages 101–108 DPP CC–DD HP Parts 3–4 *Estimated Class Sessions* **1**	**Activity** Students practice addition with two-, three-, and four-digit numbers and discover number patterns as they explore palindromes. **Math Facts** Challenge DD provides practice with multiplication facts and computation. **Homework** Assign Parts 3 and 4 of the Home Practice. **Assessment** Use the *Observational Assessment Record* to note students' abilities to add using paper and pencil.	• 1 calculator per student • colored markers or crayons • 1 set of base-ten pieces per student pair or group of three	• 1 copy of *100 Chart* URG Page 107 per student • 1 transparency of *100 Chart* URG Page 107
Lesson 8 **Digits Game** URG Pages 109–116 DAB Page 109 DPP EE–FF *Estimated Class Sessions* **1**	**Game** Students attempt to make the largest or smallest answer to addition and subtraction problems by strategically placing the digits on a playing board. **Homework** Students can play the game at home with their families. **Assessment** 1. Use the *Observational Assessment Record* to note students'abilities to add and subtract with paper and pencil. 2. Transfer appropriate assessment documentation from the Unit 6 *Observational Assessment Record* to students' *Individual Assessment Record Sheets.*	• 10 index cards per student group, optional	• 1 copy of *Digit Cards 0–9* URG Pages 115–116 copied back to back per student group • 1 copy of *Individual Assessment Record Sheet* TIG Assessment section per student, previously copied for use throughout the year

Place pattern blocks, rulers, and metersticks in a learning center for students to explore prior to beginning Unit 7.

Connections

A current list of literature and software connections is available at *www.mathtrailblazers.com*. You can also find information on connections in the *Teacher Implementation Guide* Literature List and Software List sections.

Literature Connections

Essential Titles

- Seuss, Dr. *The 500 Hats of Bartholomew Cubbins.* Random House, New York, 1989. (Lesson 1)

Suggested Titles

- Agee, Jon. *Go Hang a Salami! I'm a Lasagna Hog!* Douglas & McIntyre Ltd., Canada, 1991.
- Bergerson, Howard W. *Palindromes and Anagrams.* Dover Publications, New York, 1973. (Lesson 7)
- Cleary, Beverly. *Henry Huggins* (50th Anniversary Edition). HarperTrophy, New York, 2000. (Lesson 1)
- McKissack, Patricia C. *A Million Fish . . . More or Less.* Random House Children's Publishing, New York, 1996. (Lesson 1)
- Murphy, Stuart J. *The Shark Swimathon.* HarperCollins Publishing, New York, 2001.
- Schwartz, David M. *If You Made a Million.* HarperCollins Publishing, New York, 1989.
- Tang, Greg. *Math Appeal.* Scholastic Press, New York, 2003.
- Terban, Marvin. *Too Hot to Hoot.* Clarion Books, New York, 1985. (Lesson 7)

Software Connections

- *Carmen Sandiego's Math Detective* provides practice with math facts, estimation, ordering numbers, and word problems.
- *Discover Time* provides practice in telling time to the nearest hour, half-hour, quarter hour, and five-minute intervals.
- *Math Arena* is a collection of math activities that reinforces many math concepts.
- *Math Concepts One . . . Two . . . Three!* provides practice estimating, rounding, ordering, comparing, and writing numbers.
- *Math Munchers Deluxe* provides practice in basic facts in an arcade-like game.
- *Mighty Math Calculating Crew* poses short answer questions about number operations, three-dimensional shapes, and money skills.
- *Money Challenge* provides practice with money.
- *National Library of Virtual Manipulatives* website (http://matti.usu.edu) allows students to work with manipulatives including base-ten pieces, the abacus, and many others.
- *Numbers Recovered* provides practice comparing numeric expressions and working with place value.
- *Penny Pot* provides practice with counting coins.
- *Ten Tricky Tiles* provides practice with number facts through engaging puzzles.
- *Tenth Network: Grouping and Place Value* provides opportunities for students to group objects by twos, fives, and tens.

Teaching All Math Trailblazers Students

Math Trailblazers® lessons are designed for students with a wide range of abilities. The lessons are flexible and do not require significant adaptation for diverse learning styles or academic levels. However, when needed, lessons can be tailored to allow students to engage their abilities to the greatest extent possible while building knowledge and skills.

To assist you in meeting the needs of all students in your classroom, this section contains information about some of the features in the curriculum that allow all students access to mathematics. For additional information, see the Teaching the *Math Trailblazers* Student: Meeting Individual Needs section in the *Teacher Implementation Guide.*

Differentiation Opportunities in this Unit

Games

Use games to promote or extend understanding of math concepts and to practice skills with children who need more practice.

- Lesson 8 *Digits Game*

Journal Prompts

Journal prompts provide opportunities for students to explain and reflect on mathematical problems. They can help both students who need practice explaining their ideas and students who benefit from answering higher order questions. Students with various learning styles can express themselves using pictures, words, and sentences. Teachers can alter journal prompts to suit students' ability levels. The following lessons contain a journal prompt:

- Lesson 1 *The 500 Hats*
- Lesson 2 *The Coat of Many Bits*
- Lesson 7 *Palindromes*

DPP Challenges

DPP Challenges are items from the Daily Practice and Problems that usually take more than fifteen minutes to complete. These problems are more thought-provoking and can be used to stretch students' problem-solving skills. The following lessons have a DPP Challenge in them:

- DPP Challenge D from Lesson 2 *The Coat of Many Bits*
- DPP Challenges H and J from Lesson 3 *Adding with Base-Ten Pieces*
- DPP Challenge P from Lesson 4 *Subtracting with Base-Ten Pieces*
- DPP Challenges X and Z from Lesson 5 *Close Enough!*
- DPP Challenge DD from Lesson 7 *Palindromes*

Extensions

Use extensions to enrich lessons. Many extensions provide opportunities to further involve or challenge students of all abilities. Take a moment to review the extensions prior to beginning this unit. Some extensions may require additional preparation and planning. The following lesson contains an extension:

- Lesson 7 *Palindromes*

Unit 6

Background
More Adding and Subtracting

In this unit students' experience with two-digit addition, base-ten pieces, and a standard algorithm is extended to three- and four-digit addition. Students are introduced to subtraction with base-ten pieces and are presented with an algorithm or "shortcut" to record their work with manipulatives. Students also use base-ten pieces to find the approximate area (in square centimeters) of some large objects. These measurements then provide a context for adding and subtracting larger numbers.

The pace at which you cover the material should be determined by students' experiences. Move quickly through the algorithm work if students are already adding and subtracting with proficiency. It is, however, important to move carefully through the conceptual work with base-ten pieces. Too often, children who carry and borrow without error appear to understand the concept of place value, when in fact they have only memorized a procedure.

Using Base-Ten Pieces to Solve Subtraction Problems

Subtraction is modeled with base-ten pieces by representing the original quantity (*minuend*) on the *Base-Ten Board*. The quantity represented by the subtrahend is then removed from the board (possibly requiring regrouping first). Figure 1 provides an example.

Addition and Subtraction Algorithms

Present paper-and-pencil algorithms for addition and subtraction as shortcuts, although you should encourage students to revisit base-ten pieces as necessary to establish the connection between symbolic procedures and concrete representation. While work with base-ten pieces should inspire work with symbols, the two processes are not identical in students' minds. One major difference

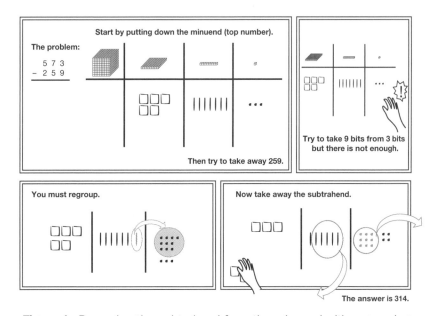

Figure 1: *Removing the subtrahend from the minuend with regrouping*

between using the pieces and the algorithm is that, with the pencil-and-paper approach, the original problem remains on the paper in some form, while with pieces, the original problem is not evident once the solution is found.

Because the link between the manipulative work and paper-and-pencil solutions is not always clear to students, some educators suggest that it is confusing to try to slavishly mimic manipulative work in a symbolic way, step-by-step—that is, doing the two procedures in parallel. Rather they recommend working the problem with pieces first and then working it symbolically. You can then make parallels between the two methods. Refer to the TIMS Tutor: *Arithmetic* for more information.

Although we discuss a particular paper-and-pencil algorithm for addition and subtraction, we are not implying that there are no other equally effective methods of solving addition and subtraction problems. For example, students in many European and Latin American countries learn a different subtraction algorithm. Allow children to explore and develop their own methods. Research shows that students who are encouraged to develop their own procedures will develop efficient methods that they understand conceptually (Wearne and Hiebert, 1994). By discussing other strategies in class, you will give credence to alternative procedures. Encourage students to share their methods with the class.

As with any procedure, students sometimes develop faulty methods. When done in a positive manner, discussions about why a method works sometimes and not other times can be very beneficial to everyone. A whole-class discussion about how to refine a nonstandard procedure helps students further develop their understanding of concepts.

Estimation

The use of estimation is found throughout the *Math Trailblazers* curriculum. In this unit, we discuss one tool used frequently when estimating the result of a computation—finding a "nice" number that is close to a given number. For example, find the sum of 57 and 74 by thinking that 57 is close

to 60 and 74 is close to 75, so the sum is close to 60 + 75. Students first work with base-ten pieces to develop their sense of numbers in relation to nice numbers such as multiples of 10 or 100. Estimation is discussed as a way of finding reasonable, close answers and a way of predicting or checking answers to computation problems.

Practice

Practice is an essential part of mathematics. Fluency with basic procedures enhances conceptual understanding of new material. It is achieved gradually over time and is maintained with regular and consistent practice. In *Math Trailblazers* the practice of addition and subtraction algorithms is implemented according to the following three considerations:

1. Practice is distributed over the curriculum. Students do short sets of problems frequently rather than many problems all at one time, especially in the Daily Practice and Problems and Home Practice.

2. Practice is embedded in problem solving in the lessons, activities, and games.

3. Students practice material already mastered while learning new content.

This program of practice allows teachers to monitor students' use of computation strategies as they are being developed. Teachers can quickly identify incorrect procedures and help students use correct ones before they become ingrained.

Resources

- Hiebert, J. "Relationships between Research and the NCTM Standards." *Journal for Research in Mathematics Education,* 30 (1), pp. 3–19, 1999.

- National Research Council. "Developing Proficiency with Whole Numbers." In *Adding It Up: Helping Children Learn Mathematics.* J. Kilpatrick, J. Swafford, and B. Findell, Eds.: National Academy Press, Washington, DC, 2001.

- National Research Council. "Teaching for Mathematical Proficiency." In *Adding It Up: Helping Children Learn Mathematics.* J. Kilpatrick, J. Swafford, and B. Findell, Eds.: National Academy Press, Washington, DC, 2001.

- Wearne, Diana, and James Hiebert. "Place Value and Addition and Subtraction." *Arithmetic Teacher,* 41(5), pp. 272–274, 1994.

Observational Assessment Record

(A1) Can students represent addition and subtraction using base-ten pieces?
(A2) Can students add multidigit numbers using paper and pencil?
(A3) Can students subtract multidigit numbers using paper and pencil?
(A4) Can students estimate sums and differences?
(A5) Can students determine the reasonableness of a solution?
(A6) Can students solve problems involving addition and subtraction?
(A7) _____

Name	A1	A2	A3	A4	A5	A6	A7	Comments
1.								
2.								
3.								
4.								
5.								
6.								
7.								
8.								
9.								
10.								
11.								
12.								
13.								

Name	A1	A2	A3	A4	A5	A6	A7	Comments
14.								
15.								
16.								
17.								
18.								
19.								
20.								
21.								
22.								
23.								
24.								
25.								
26.								
27.								
28.								
29.								
30.								
31.								
32.								

Unit 6

Daily Practice and Problems
More Adding and Subtracting

A DPP Menu for Unit 6

Two Daily Practice and Problems (DPP) items are included for each class session listed in the Unit Outline. A scope and sequence chart for the DPP is in the *Teacher Implementation Guide*.

Icons in the Teacher Notes column designate the subject matter of each DPP item. The first item in each class session is always a Bit and the second is either a Task or Challenge. Each item falls into one or more of the categories listed below. A menu of the DPP items for Unit 6 follows.

N Number Sense	Computation	Time	Geometry
B–D, H, K, M, N, P, R, S, X–Z, AA, EE, FF	C, E, G, J, L, N, R, T, U, W–Y, AA–FF	A, I, L, O, Q, R, T	
Math Facts	$ Money	Measurement	Data
B–D, F, H, V, DD	G, P, W, DD	BB	

Practicing the Subtraction Facts

This unit is a time for students to review all the subtraction facts, Groups 1–8. They studied all the facts two groups at a time in Units 2–5. Flash cards were distributed in each unit in the *Discovery Assignment Book* following the Home Practice. Students will take short quizzes on these facts in Units 7–10. In Unit 10 you will administer a *Subtraction Fact Inventory* of all the subtraction facts.

Students should continue practicing the facts using their flash cards and updating their *Subtraction Facts I Know* charts. Unit 6 focuses on addition and subtraction of multidigit numbers. Therefore, practice of the addition and subtraction facts takes place primarily as part of the lessons rather than the DPP.

Developing Strategies for the Multiplication Facts

DPP items in this unit develop strategies for the multiplication facts for the nines. See DPP items B, F, V, and DD for work with these facts.

For information on the practice and assessment of subtraction facts in Grade 3, see the Lesson Guide for Unit 2 Lesson 7 *Assessing the Subtraction Facts*. For information on the study of the multiplication facts in Grade 3, see the Daily Practice and Problems Guide for Unit 11. For a detailed explanation of our approach to learning and assessing the math facts in Grade 3, see the *Grade 3 Facts Resource Guide,* and for information for Grades K–5, see the TIMS Tutor: *Math Facts* in the *Teacher Implementation Guide.*

Daily Practice and Problems

Students may solve the items individually, in groups, or as a class. The items may also be assigned for homework. The DPPs are also available on the Teacher Resource CD.

Student Questions	Teacher Notes
A **Time**	**TIMS Bit**
What time is it now?	Answers depend on the time of day.
What time will it be in half an hour?	
What time was it 15 minutes ago?	
B **Guess My Number Puzzles**	**TIMS Task**
1. I am more than 3×9 and less than 4×9. I am odd. The sum of my digits is 4. Who am I?	1. 31
	2. 45
	3. 13
2. The sum of my digits is nine. If you skip count by 5s, you hit me. Who am I?	
3. I am odd. I am more than half of 22 and less than half of 30. Who am I?	

Subtraction: Using Doubles

Do the following problems in your head. Write only the answers.

1. 50 − 25 =

2. 51 − 25 =

3. 100 − 50 =

4. 100 − 48 =

5. 180 − 90 =

6. 160 − 80 =

7. Explain your strategy for Question 4.

TIMS Bit

These problems can be solved by thinking addition with doubles. (Since 25 + 25 = 50, then 50 − 25 = 25.) However, students will probably solve them in many ways. Ask them to describe their strategies, helping them verbalize their thinking.

1. 25
2. 26
3. 50
4. 52
5. 90
6. 80

7. Possible strategy: Students may count up from 48 to 50 and then use the double 50 + 50 to find the missing part.

 School Clothes

Jerry likes to wear T-shirts and shorts to school. He has three T-shirts: a red one, a blue one, and a white one. He has two pairs of shorts: a blue pair and a black pair. How many different outfits does Jerry have for school?

TIMS Challenge

6 outfits:

Shirts	Shorts
red	blue
red	black
blue	blue
blue	black
white	blue
white	black

E Goo the Glob

Boo the Blob's cousin, Goo the Glob, has three times as much area as Boo the Blob. What is the area of Goo the Glob?

If the two cousins sit beside each other at a family dinner, what is their total area?

TIMS Bit

Students found the area of Boo the Blob to be about 20 sq cm in Unit 5.

Since Boo the Blob has an area of about 20 sq cm, Goo has an area of 3×20, or 60 sq cm.

The total area of the two cousins is $60 + 20$, or 80 sq cm.

F Multiplication Strategies

Dima says that he finds 6×9 this way, "I think 6 tens are 60, so 6 nines will be 6 less." $6 \times 10 = 60$ and $60 - 6 = 54$.

1. Use Dima's strategy to find 2×9.

2. Use his strategy to find 7×9.

3. Find 9×9.

TIMS Task

1. $2 \times 10 = 20$ and
   $20 - 2 = 18$

2. $7 \times 10 = 70$ and
   $70 - 7 = 63$

3. 81

G Change

Jade bought a box of juice for 39¢. She paid with a $1 bill. How much change did she get?

What coins could she receive in change?

Can you find more than one solution?

TIMS Bit

Change: 61¢

There are many possible solutions. Here are three:

2 quarters, 1 dime, 1 penny

2 quarters, 2 nickels, 1 penny

6 dimes, 1 penny

Cold Cafe

The Cold Cafe is an ice cream parlor. The cafe has three kinds of cones: plain, sugar, and waffle. There are four flavors of ice cream: chocolate, vanilla, strawberry, and mint. How many different one-scoop cones can you get?

TIMS Challenge

Solution: 12 cones

Students can draw pictures or make diagrams to solve the problems.

Plain: Ch, Van, Str, Mt

Waffle: Ch, Van, Str, Mt

Sugar Ch, Van, Str, Mt

 Late for School

Lem is always late for school. It takes him 20 minutes to walk to school. If school starts at 8:15 A.M., what time should he leave to be on time?

TIMS Bit

Lem must leave for school no later than 7:55 A.M.

 Bicycle Riding

James likes to ride his bicycle. He rides two miles every day after school. He rides five miles each weekend day.

1. How far does he ride in one week?

2. How long will it take James to ride 100 miles?

TIMS Challenge

1. He rides 20 miles in one week.
   2 + 2 + 2 + 2 + 2 + 5 + 5 = 20.

2. It will take him 5 weeks.

mi: 20 40 60 80 100

wks: 1 2 3 4 5

 Counting Backwards

1. Count backwards from 20 to 0 by ones.

2. Count backwards from 100 to 0 by tens.

3. Count backwards from 200 to 100 by tens.

TIMS Bit

A student can write the numbers on the board as the class counts.

L **More Bicycle Riding**

Elly rides her bicycle 4 miles every day. How many days will it take her to ride 100 miles?

How many weeks?

TIMS Task

Elly will take 25 days to ride 100 miles. Students can skip count by 4s on the calculator, counting the number of skips until they reach 100.

25 days is between 3 weeks and 4 weeks.

 M **Calculator Counting Starting at 5**

Use your calculator to count.

A. Start at 5 and count by 10s to 200. Press $5 + 10 = = = = \ldots$ Count quietly to yourself. Describe any patterns you see. Can you stop exactly on 200?

B. Start at 5 and count by 9s to 200. Press $5 + 9 = = = = \ldots$ Count quietly to yourself. Describe any patterns you see. Can you stop exactly on 200?

TIMS Bit

The pattern in Problem B will be used to solve problems adding and subtracting 9 in the following item.

As students count by nines, they are adding nine to the previous number. Each time 9 is added, the number in the ones place decreases by 1 and the number in the 10s place increases by 1 until the number in the ones place reaches 0.

Then, adding a 9 puts a 9 in the ones place, and the pattern begins again.

 N **Adding Nine**

Write the following problems on a piece of paper, then solve them. Look for patterns.

1. $14 + 9 =$ 2. $104 + 9 =$ 3. $41 + 9 =$

4. $23 + 9 =$ 5. $32 + 9 =$ 6. $42 + 9 =$

7. $77 + 9 =$ 8. $68 + 9 =$ 9. $95 + 9 =$

TIMS Task

Discuss possible strategies for finding the answers to these problems. Compare the patterns students described in the previous bit to the patterns found when adding 9.

1. 23	2. 113	3. 50
4. 32	5. 41	6. 51
7. 86	8. 77	9. 104

Student Questions	Teacher Notes

 Past, Present, and Future

What is the date today?

What will the date be in 9 days?

What was the date 9 days ago?

TIMS Bit

Answers will vary depending on the date.

 Change for $1

How many ways can you make change for $1 using only nickels and dimes? Prove your answer.

TIMS Challenge

A table or chart may help students organize their thinking.

There are 11 ways:

Nickels	Dimes
0 nickels	10 dimes
2 nickels	9 dimes
4 nickels	8 dimes
6 nickels	7 dimes
8 nickels	6 dimes
10 nickels	5 dimes
12 nickels	4 dimes
14 nickels	3 dimes
16 nickels	2 dimes
18 nickels	1 dimes
20 nickels	0 dimes

 Past, Present, and Future Again

What is the day of the week today?

What day will it be in 9 days?

What day was it 9 days ago?

How did you find your answers?

TIMS Bit

Answers will vary depending on the day of the week.

Inventions

1. The first zipper was invented in 1893. About how many years ago was the zipper invented? Exactly how many years?

2. The first wooden pencils were square. They were invented in 1683. Rounded pencils were invented in 1876. How long did people use square pencils before round ones were invented? Is your answer reasonable?

TIMS Task

1. The first zipper was invented about 100 years ago. The exact number of years will vary depending on the current year.

2.   1876
   −1683
   ─────
    193 years

Since 1876 and 1683 are about 200 years apart, then 193 is reasonable.

 Basketball Points

In 1962, Wilt Chamberlain scored a total of 4029 points in games. In 1970, Jerry West scored 2309 points. In 1992, Michael Jordan scored 2404 points. Put the number of total points for these players in order from smallest to largest. You may use base-ten pieces to help you.

TIMS Bit

2309, 2404, 4029

 Time

1. How many minutes are in $1\frac{1}{2}$ hours?

2. It takes Karen $\frac{1}{2}$ hour to wash the dishes. If she washes dishes every night for a week, how many minutes will she spend washing the dishes? How many hours?

TIMS Task

1. 90 minutes

2. 210 minutes, $3\frac{1}{2}$ hours

Student Questions	Teacher Notes

 Shortcut Addition

Do the following problems using a shortcut method. You may use base-ten shorthand if you wish.

1. 76
    $+\ 27$

2. 617
    $+\ 75$

3. 159
    $+ 345$

4. 809
    $+ 151$

5. Explain another strategy for answering Question 4.

TIMS Bit

1. 103

2. 692

3. 504

4. 960

5. Possible strategy: Students may recognize that $9 + 1 = 10$ and convert the problem to $810 + 150 = 960$.

 Story Solving

Write a story and draw a picture about 8×9. Write a number sentence on your picture.

TIMS Task

Stories will vary.

 More Change

1. How much change from $1.00 do you get if you pay 79¢ for a folder?

2. How much change from $5.00 do you get if you pay $1.79 for a hamburger?

TIMS Bit

1. 21¢

Students may choose to "count up" to find the answer: Count up 1¢ to 80¢ then 20¢ to $1.
$20¢ + 1¢ = 21¢$

2. $3.21

Students may choose to "count up" to find the answer: Count up 21¢ as shown above to $2; then, count up $3 to $5.

Addition Squares

Draw boxes on your paper like these. Fill in the boxes using the digits 5, 6, 7, and 8. Use each digit only once.

☐ ☐ + ☐ ☐ =

1. What is the largest sum you can get?

2. What is the smallest sum you can get?

3. How many different sums can you find?

TIMS Challenge

The largest sum is 161 = 76 + 85 or 86 + 75 = 161. The smallest sum is 125 = 57 + 68 or 67 + 58 = 125.

There are 24 different addition problems that generate 5 different sums. The sums are 125, 134, 143, 152, and 161.

 Forest Fires

On an average day, 166 forest fires start. Lightning starts 85 of these fires. How many are started by something other than lightning?

Are more than half the fires started by lightning?

TIMS Bit

166 − 85 = 81

Yes, more than half the fires are started by lightning.

 Books

Estimate how many books are in your classroom right now. Explain how you came up with your estimate.

TIMS Challenge

Encourage students to make a plan for finding a reasonable estimate. They may need to count the number of books in several desks or the number of books on a shelf, but they should not need to count them all. Compare students' strategies for estimating the number of books in the room. Is one more accurate than another? Is one more efficient than another?

Compare the estimates. Is there only one correct answer? If there is not one right answer, can an answer be wrong?

Student Questions	**Teacher Notes**

 Shortcut Subtraction

Do the following problems using a shortcut method. You can use base-ten shorthand if you want.

1. 147
   − 36

2. 563
   − 125

3. 2750
   − 129

4. 5007
   − 4997

5. Explain a way to do Question 4 in your head.

TIMS Bit

1. 111
2. 438
3. 2621
4. 10
5. Possible strategy: If students count up from 4997, they should realize that the difference is 10.

 Measuring Ourselves

Find a partner. Measure to find out how tall you and your partner are in centimeters.

1. Who is taller? How much taller?

2. If you stood on your partner's shoulders, how tall would you both be?

TIMS Task

Answers will vary according to the students' heights. Did students take into account that one of the partner's heads will not be included in the sum in the second question?

CC **More Raincoats**

Joe the Goldfish has two cousins, Zelda the Zebra Fish and Angie the Angel Fish. Zelda has a raincoat made with 1793 sq cm of material. Angie's raincoat is 288 sq cm bigger than Zelda's.

Did it take more than 2000 sq cm of material to make Angie's raincoat?

What is the exact area of Angie's raincoat?

TIMS Bit

Angie's raincoat is more than 2000 sq cm.

1793 + 288 = 2081 sq cm

Jonah's Class Project

Jonah's class is recycling aluminum cans to raise money for a field trip. If he finds 9 cans a day for an entire week, how many cans will he have for his class?

The class needs $3 more to pay for the bus. If Jonah receives 5 cents for each can he collected during the week, will they have enough?

TIMS Challenge

Jonah will have 63 cans by the end of the week. The 63 cans will earn his class $3.15. Therefore, they will have the money they need to rent the bus.

To find the number of cans, students might skip count by nines.

cans: 9 18 27 36 45 54 63

days: 1   2   3   4   5   6   7

To find out how much money he earned students might use a calculator or repeated addition.
$63 + 63 + 63 + 63 + 63 = 315$

 Play Digits: Largest Sum

As your teacher or classmate reads the digits, place them in the boxes. Try to find the largest sum. Remember, each digit will be read only once.

TIMS Bit

The directions for Play Digits are in *Digits Game* in Lesson 8. Students should use the digits 0–9.

 Play Digits: Largest and Smallest Difference

Draw boxes on your paper like these:

As your teacher or classmate reads the digits, place them in the boxes. Try to find the smallest difference. Remember each digit will be read only once.

Play again, but this time find the largest difference.

TIMS Task

The directions for Play Digits are in *Digits Game* in Lesson 8. Students should use the digits 0–9.

Lesson 1

The 500 Hats

Estimated Class Sessions

1

Lesson Overview

The 500 Hats of Bartholomew Cubbins by Dr. Seuss provides a context for the continued development of students' addition and subtraction strategies with multidigit numbers. Students partition, add, and subtract two- and three-digit numbers using mental strategies. They are then asked to make up problems based on the story.

Key Content

- Developing number sense.
- Adding and subtracting multidigit numbers.
- Developing mental math skills.
- Connecting mathematics and language arts.

Math Facts

DPP Task B provides practice with multiplication facts for the nines.

Homework

1. Students can write other stories with addition and subtraction problems.
2. Assign Part 1 of the Home Practice.

Assessment

Use the *Observational Assessment Record* to note students' abilities to solve problems involving addition and subtraction using mental strategies.

Materials List

Supplies and Copies

Student	Teacher
Supplies for Each Student • calculator, optional **Supplies for Each Student Pair or Group of Three** • 1 set of base-ten pieces: 2 packs, 14 flats, 30 skinnies, and 50 bits	**Supplies** • *The 500 Hats of Bartholomew Cubbins* by Dr. Seuss or another story that refers to numbers in the hundreds
Copies	**Copies/Transparencies** • 1 copy of *Observational Assessment Record* to be used throughout this unit (*Unit Resource Guide* Pages 13–14)

All blackline masters including assessment, transparency, and DPP masters are also on the Teacher Resource CD.

Daily Practice and Problems and Home Practice

DPP items A–B (*Unit Resource Guide* Page 16)
Home Practice Part 1 (*Discovery Assignment Book* Page 100)

Note: Classrooms whose pacing differs significantly from the suggested pacing of the units should use the Math Facts Calendar in Section 4 of the *Facts Resource Guide* to ensure students receive the complete math facts program.

Assessment Tools

Observational Assessment Record (*Unit Resource Guide* Pages 13–14)

Daily Practice and Problems

Suggestions for using the DPPs are on page 30.

A. Bit: Time (URG p. 16)

What time is it now?

What time will it be in half an hour?

What time was it 15 minutes ago?

B. Task: Guess My Number Puzzles
(URG p. 16)

1. I am more than 3 × 9 and less than 4 × 9. I am odd. The sum of my digits is 4. Who am I?
2. The sum of my digits is nine. If you skip count by 5s, you hit me. Who am I?
3. I am odd. I am more than half of 22 and less than half of 30. Who am I?

Before the Activity

This lesson is written to be used with *The 500 Hats of Bartholomew Cubbins.* If you do not have access to this particular book or if you prefer another story, substitute other books that provide contexts for addition and subtraction problems with two- and three-digit numbers. The chapter entitled "Gallons of Guppies" in *Henry Huggins* by Beverly Cleary is one of many such examples.

Teaching the Activity

The lesson revolves around the story *The 500 Hats of Bartholomew Cubbins* by Dr. Seuss. In the story a boy named Bartholomew had trouble removing his hat to honor the king. Whenever he took one hat off, another hat immediately appeared on his head. Bartholomew was taken to the king's castle, where repeated attempts to remove Bartholomew's hats were thwarted by new hats appearing. The 500th hat that appeared on Bartholomew's head was decorated with huge feathers and jewels. The king offered to buy this hat. After removing this beautiful hat, no other hat appeared on Bartholomew's head. Throughout the adventure, a scribe keeps track of the number of hats that have appeared on Bartholomew's head, providing numerous opportunities to investigate operations with two- and three-digit numbers.

As you read or tell the story to your class, pose problems such as:

- *When Sir Alaric says that 154 hats had already come off, how many hats had come off since the king had called for Sir Snipps, the hat maker?*

- *When Bartholomew says that the executioner had knocked off 13 hats and that he had left 178 more on the dungeon steps, how many hats was he talking about altogether?*

- *When the hats begin to change, 450 hats had already come off. Based on the book's title, how many hats are left on Bartholomew's head?*

Make up problems that refer to the story's plot. For example:

- *When he had taken off 275 hats, how many more hats would eventually appear on his head?*

- *If 45 hats blew off before he got to the castle, and 205 more came off before he reached the dungeon, how many hats had he lost?*

- *At one point Bartholomew said he had thrown off 180 hats while in the turret. If he had already lost 150 hats in other places, how many hats had he lost at this point?*

- *When Bartholomew left the turret, he had lost a total of 330 hats. If he lost 160 hats while he was in the turret, how many hats had he lost before entering the turret?*

Emphasize partitioning numbers and using mental strategies, such as partitioning and combining, doubling, using complements of ten and a hundred, or skip counting.

Encourage students to write number sentences to describe the different problems. Base-ten pieces should be made available for students to keep track of the numbers in their solutions. Do not discourage students from using pencil-and-paper algorithms to solve any problems. Keep in mind, however, that the goal of this activity is to engage students in using their own strategies to add and subtract numbers rather than to teach them formal procedures. Give students ample opportunity to share their strategies for solving problems with the class.

Ask students to make up their own addition and subtraction problems based on the story. In addition to problems related to the story, some students are likely to come up with problems that are only indirectly connected to the story's plot but are still valuable for classroom discussion.

Journal Prompt

Write a story about somebody who has an adventure involving 500 of something. Make up and solve several math problems about your story.

Unit 6 Home Practice

PART 1

1. A. $15 - 9 =$ _____   B. $17 - 10 =$ _____

   C. $9 - 4 =$ _____   D. $11 - 7 =$ _____

   E. $7 - 2 =$ _____   F. $12 - 3 =$ _____

   G. $14 - 8 =$ _____   H. $18 - 9 =$ _____

2. Leah has a hard time finding the answer to 1G. How did you find the answer to this subtraction fact? Share your method.

PART 2

1. Solve the addition and subtraction problems. Show how you solved each one.

   A. $156 + 54 =$ _____   B. $232 - 29 =$ _____

2. Sharon works at a flower shop. She received a shipment of roses and carnations. She received 48 roses. She received 60 more carnations than roses. Show how you solved the following problems.

   A. How many carnations did she receive? _____

   B. How many flowers did she receive in all? _____

100 DAB • Grade 3 • Unit 6   MORE ADDING AND SUBTRACTING

Discovery Assignment Book - page 100 (Answers on p. 32)

Math Facts

- DPP Task B provides practice with the multiplication facts for the nines.
- Part 1 of the Home Practice provides practice with subtraction facts.

Homework and Practice

- Ask students to write and solve addition and subtraction problems based on this story or another story of their choice as homework. Students should show how they solved these problems.
- You can also use the Journal Prompt as a homework assignment.
- DPP Bit A provides practice telling time.
- Assign Part 1 of the Home Practice in the *Discovery Assignment Book*.

Answers for Part 1 of the Home Practice are in the Answer Key at the end of this lesson and at the end of this unit.

Assessment

Use class discussion and homework to assess students' abilities to solve addition and subtraction problems using number sense and mental strategies. Record your observations in the *Observational Assessment Record*.

Literature Connections

- Cleary, Beverly. *Henry Huggins.* (50th Anniversary Edition). HarperTrophy, New York, 2000.
- McKissack, Patricia C. *A Million Fish . . . More or Less.* Random House Children's Publishing, New York, 1996.
- Seuss, Dr. *The 500 Hats of Bartholomew Cubbins.* Random House, New York, 1989.

Math Facts and Daily Practice and Problems

DPP Bit A provides practice telling time. Task B provides practice with multiplication facts for the nines.

Teaching the Activity

1. Students listen to a story *The 500 Hats of Bartholomew Cubbins* by Dr. Seuss.
2. Students solve problems based on the story using their own strategies.
3. Students make up their own problems based on the story and write them in their journals.

Homework

1. Students can write other stories with addition and subtraction problems.
2. Assign Part 1 of the Home Practice.

Assessment

Use the *Observational Assessment Record* to note students' abilities to solve problems involving addition and subtraction using mental strategies.

Connections

Read and discuss *Henry Huggins* by Beverly Cleary, *A Million Fish . . . More or Less* by Patricia C. McKissack, or *The 500 Hats of Bartholomew Cubbins* by Dr. Seuss.

Answer Key is on page 32.

Notes:

Name _____ Date _____

Unit 6 Home Practice

PART 1

1. A. 15 − 9 = _____   B. 17 − 10 = _____
   C. 9 − 4 = _____   D. 11 − 7 = _____
   E. 7 − 2 = _____   F. 12 − 3 = _____
   G. 14 − 8 = _____   H. 18 − 9 = _____

2. Leah has a hard time finding the answer to 1G. How did you find the answer to this subtraction fact? Share your method.

PART 2

1. Solve the addition and subtraction problems. Show how you solved each one.
   A. 156 + 54 = _____   B. 232 − 29 = _____

2. Sharon works at a flower shop. She received a shipment of roses and carnations. She received 48 roses. She received 60 more carnations than roses. Show how you solved the following problems.

   A. How many carnations did she receive? _____

   B. How many flowers did she receive in all? _____

100 DAB • Grade 3 • Unit 6   MORE ADDING AND SUBTRACTING

Discovery Assignment Book - page 100

Discovery Assignment Book (p. 100)

Home Practice*

Part 1

1. **A.** 6   **B.** 7
   C. 5   **D.** 4
   E. 5   **F.** 9
   G. 6   **H.** 9

2. Strategies will vary. One possible strategy is to use doubles; 14 is the double of 7. Since 8 is one more than 7, the answer will be one less, or 6.

---

*Answers for all the Home Practice in the *Discovery Assignment Book* are at the end of the unit.

The Coat of Many Bits

Lesson Overview

Estimated Class Sessions **2-3**

Students trace an outline of their coats or jackets onto a large sheet of paper and measure the area inside the outline. The data collected through these measurements tends to be "big" (i.e., four-digit) numbers that are then used in problem situations.

Key Content

- Measuring the area of irregular shapes in square centimeters.
- Understanding place value.
- Using base-ten pieces to add.
- Comparing and ordering four-digit numbers.
- Estimating sums and differences using benchmarks.

Math Facts

DPP items C, D, and F provide practice with math facts.

Homework

Students complete *Questions 5–7* on *The Coat of Many Bits* Activity Page.

Materials List

Supplies and Copies

Student	Teacher
Supplies for Each Student Group • student's coat; a jacket, sweater, or sweatshirt may be substituted for the coat • large sheet of paper at least 2 yards by 1 yard • index card • crayons • scissors • tape **Supplies for Each Student Pair or Group of Three** • 1 set of base-ten pieces without packs: 14 flats, 30 skinnies, and 50 bits	**Supplies**
Copies	**Copies/Transparencies**

All blackline masters including assessment, transparency, and DPP masters are also on the Teacher Resource CD.

Student Books

The Coat of Many Bits (*Student Guide* Page 66)

Daily Practice and Problems and Home Practice

DPP items C–F (*Unit Resource Guide* Pages 17–18)

Note: Classrooms whose pacing differs significantly from the suggested pacing of the units should use the Math Facts Calendar in Section 4 of the *Facts Resource Guide* to ensure students receive the complete math facts program.

Daily Practice and Problems

Suggestions for using the DPPs are on page 38.

C. Bit: Subtraction:
    Using Doubles (URG p. 17)

Do the following problems in your head. Write only the answers.

1. $50 - 25 =$ 2. $51 - 25 =$
3. $100 - 50 =$ 4. $100 - 48 =$
5. $180 - 90 =$ 6. $160 - 80 =$
7. Explain your strategy for Question 4.

D. Challenge: School Clothes
    (URG p. 17)

Jerry likes to wear T-shirts and shorts to school. He has three T-shirts: a red one, a blue one, and a white one. He has two pairs of shorts: a blue pair and a black pair. How many different outfits does Jerry have for school?

E. Bit: Goo the Glob (URG p. 18)

Boo the Blob's cousin, Goo the Glob, has three times as much area as Boo the Blob. What is the area of Goo the Glob?

If the two cousins sit beside each other at a family dinner, what is their total area?

F. Task: Multiplication Strategies
    (URG p. 18)

Dima says that he finds 6×9 this way, "I think 6 tens are 60, so 6 nines will be 6 less." $6 \times 10 = 60$ and $60 - 6 = 54$.

1. Use Dima's strategy to find 2×9.
2. Use his strategy to find 7×9.
3. Find 9×9.

The Coat of Many Bits

Making Costumes for a Play

Help wanted! Your creative talents are needed to help make costumes for the school play "Michael and the Land of Many Colors." The students want to cover the front of the costumes with a special, colorful material. They need your help in figuring out how much of this material they will need. To do this, your group will need one coat.

1. Trace the outline of the coat onto a large piece of paper.

2. Use base-ten pieces to find out how much material (in square centimeters) will be needed to cover the front of the coat. Use any shortcuts that will save time in finding this area.

3. Write the area of your coat on a piece of paper or an index card.

4. Make a list of the areas of all of the coats in the class. Order them from smallest to largest.

5. Do the problems below. Make sure that your answers are reasonable.
   A. About how much bigger is the largest coat than the smallest coat?
   B. Is it more or less than 500 square centimeters bigger?
   C. Is it more or less than 1000 square centimeters bigger?

6. The material costs 10¢ for every 100 square centimeters. How much will it cost to cover your group's coat? Show how you found your answer.

7. When you made your costumes, your group started with a big piece of material. You then cut out just enough material to cover your group's coat. Let's say the original piece of material had a total area of 6000 square centimeters. About how much would be left over after you cut out enough material to cover your group's coat?

The Coat of Many Bits

Student Guide - page 66 *(Answers on p. 40)*

Journal Prompt

Why are bits, skinnies, and flats appropriate for measuring area but packs are not?

Cut sheets of butcher paper into pieces large enough for students to lay a coat or jacket on and trace the entire outline. About 2 yards by 1 yard is usually adequate.

Teaching the Activity

The Coat of Many Bits Activity Page in the *Student Guide* describes the context for the lesson. A group of students are producing a play entitled "Michael and the Land of Many Colors." Your students will assist with the production by helping to make the costumes. Other aspects of the play become the topic of mathematical explorations in a later activity.

The activity page explains that the front of the costumes will be covered with a fancy, colorful material. To do this, students first trace the outline of a coat on a large sheet of paper. This gives them a picture (or model) of the coat. They use this picture to find out how much material they need to cover the front.

In Unit 5 students measured area by tracing shapes on centimeter grids and counting square centimeters. In this activity they count square centimeters using base-ten pieces. Ask students how they could use base-ten pieces to estimate the area of the front of their coats. If necessary, point out that the different sizes of base-ten pieces cover a different number of square centimeters—one bit covers one square centimeter—therefore a skinny covers ten square centimeters, and a flat covers 100 square centimeters.

Model the activity by tracing the outline of a student's coat on the board (with the help of a couple of students).

There are several practical points to discuss, such as:

• Each group will only find the area of one coat; this will be the group's coat.

• The coats should be zipped (or snapped or buttoned) and the sleeves should be extended.

• Hoods of coats should not be included since only the fronts of the coats will be covered with fancy material.

• The coats should be held flat against the surfaces they are traced on.

• Do not use markers when tracing because they may stain the coats.

Covering the *entire* outline with base-ten pieces is time-consuming. Encourage students to use their knowledge of symmetry to make the measuring go faster. Ask students whether it is possible to measure only part of the coat yet find the area of the whole thing. Students should realize that measuring the right or left half is sufficient because the coat is symmetrical around the zipper (snaps or buttons).

For this activity, students should work in groups no larger than three. We recommend that students trace the outlines of the base-ten pieces on the picture of their coats and figure out the area afterwards. See Figure 2. This way, students have a permanent record of their work and can continue the activity if it is interrupted. Note that there will be some error in their measurements because the pieces will not *perfectly* cover the picture. This should be discussed at some point during the lesson.

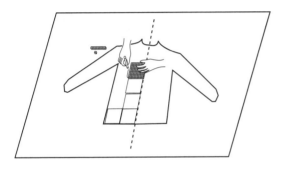

Figure 2: *Making outlines around the base-ten pieces*

Ask students to cut out their coat outline when they finish tracing the base-ten pieces. If students only find the area of half the coat, all written work can be done on the blank half. (It can be done on the back if students cover the entire coat with base-ten pieces.) In most cases, for half a coat, students will find that they have 10 or more of each of the flats, skinnies, and bits. This requires them to interpret that, for example, 22 flats, 19 skinnies, and 54 bits are the same as 2200 bits, 190 bits, and 54 bits, or 2444. The final answer should be in square centimeters. Remind students to report the area of the coat's whole front, not just the half they measured with base-ten pieces.

TIMS Tip

This activity requires a lot of floor space for students to spread out the coats, so you may need to reserve a larger room or use the hallway.

Ask each group to record the area of their coat on an index card. Place all the cards on a bulletin or poster board that is accessible to students. In *Question 4* on *The Coat of Many Bits* Activity Page, students are asked to order the areas from smallest to largest. This can be done as a whole-class activity. Students place their own index cards in the order they think is appropriate. Discuss how students made their decisions, particularly if there are differences of opinion as to order. If they have difficulty with this, more practice is provided later in the unit. Students can verify their ordered areas with visual models. Distribute base-ten packs for this purpose.

Tape the cutout coats to the board in the order students arranged the areas. The coat sizes should appear to be in order from smallest to largest. Ask students for suggestions to explain any big discrepancies. Students may have measured the area incorrectly, they may have doubled incorrectly, or they may have ordered the areas incorrectly.

After completing the data collection, students should do *Questions 5–7* on *The Coat of Many Bits* Activity Page. In *Question 5* the emphasis is on comparing numbers with benchmarks, such as 500, 1000, 5000, 10,000, and so on, not on computing exact solutions. Students need to think about and discuss what parts of the numbers are the most important in estimation problems like these. For example, should they examine the tens, hundreds, or the thousands first?

Math Facts

DPP items C, D, and F provide practice with math facts. Bit C is subtraction with ending zeros. Task F develops strategies for the multiplication facts.

Homework and Practice

- You can assign *Questions 5–7* on *The Coat of Many Bits* Activity Page for homework.
- DPP Bit E is a computation problem.

Math Facts and Daily Practice and Problems

DPP items C, D, and F provide practice with math facts. Bit E practices computation.

Teaching the Activity

1. Students read *The Coat of Many Bits* Activity Page in the *Student Guide.*
2. Students trace a coat onto a large sheet of paper.
3. Students use base-ten pieces to find the area of their coat.
4. Students cut out the paper coat.
5. Students write the area of their coat onto an index card.
6. Students order the areas of all the coats from smallest area to largest area.
7. Students post cutout coats in order, from smallest to largest area.
8. Students verify whether their areas are correct and in order.

Homework

Students complete *Questions 5–7* on *The Coat of Many Bits* Activity Page.

Answer Key is on page 40.

Notes:

The Coat of Many Bits

Making Costumes for a Play

Help wanted! Your creative talents are needed to help make costumes for the school play "Michael and the Land of Many Colors." The students want to cover the front of the costumes with a special, colorful material. They need your help in figuring out how much of this material they will need. To do this, your group will need one coat.

1. Trace the outline of the coat onto a large piece of paper.

2. Use base-ten pieces to find out how much material (in square centimeters) will be needed to cover the front of the coat. Use any shortcuts that will save time in finding this area.

3. Write the area of your coat on a piece of paper or an index card.

4. Make a list of the areas of all of the coats in the class. Order them from smallest to largest.

5. Do the problems below. Make sure that your answers are reasonable.
   A. About how much bigger is the largest coat than the smallest coat?
   B. Is it more or less than 500 square centimeters bigger?
   C. Is it more or less than 1000 square centimeters bigger?

6. The material costs 10¢ for every 100 square centimeters. How much will it cost to cover your group's coat? Show how you found your answer.

7. When you made your costumes, your group started with a big piece of material. You then cut out just enough material to cover your group's coat. Let's say the original piece of material had a total area of 6000 square centimeters. About how much would be left over after you cut out enough material to cover your group's coat?

 SG • Grade 3 • Unit 6 • Lesson 2   The Coat of Many Bits

Student Guide - page 66

Student Guide (p. 66)

Answers are dependent upon students' data.*

*Answers and/or discussion are included in the Lesson Guide.

Lesson 3

Adding with Base-Ten Pieces

Lesson Overview

Estimated Class Sessions

3-4

Children expand their understanding of place value and continue to explore addition with base-ten pieces.

Key Content

- Understanding place value.
- Representing addition using base-ten pieces.
- Developing an addition algorithm.
- Adding using paper and pencil.

Key Vocabulary

- Fewest Pieces Rule

Math Facts

DPP Challenge H provides practice with multiplication facts.

Homework

1. Assign **Questions 3–6** on the *Adding on the Base-Ten Board* Activity Pages in the *Discovery Assignment Book* after Part 1.
2. Assign the Homework section in the *Student Guide* after Part 2.
3. Assign Part 2 of the Home Practice for more practice with addition and subtraction.

Assessment

Use the *Observational Assessment Record* to note students' progress representing addition using base-ten pieces.

Curriculum Sequence

Before This Unit

Students represented addition of two-digit numbers using base-ten pieces in Grade 3 Unit 4 Lesson 3.

After This Unit

Students will practice addition and subtraction of multidigit numbers in the Daily Practice and Problems, Home Practice, and in the context of a reading survey in Unit 14.

Materials List

Supplies and Copies

Student	Teacher
Supplies for Each Student Pair or Group of Three • 1 set of base-ten pieces: 2 packs, 14 flats, 30 skinnies, and 50 bits	**Supplies**
Copies • 1 copy of *Base-Ten Board* per student pair (*Unit Resource Guide* Pages 51–52) • 1 copy of *Base-Ten Recording Sheet* per student (*Unit Resource Guide* Page 53)	**Copies/Transparencies** • 1 transparency of *Base-Ten Board*, optional (*Unit Resource Guide* Pages 51–52) • 1 transparency of *Base-Ten Recording Sheet,* optional (*Unit Resource Guide* Page 53)

All blackline masters including assessment, transparency, and DPP masters are also on the Teacher Resource CD.

Student Books
Adding with Base-Ten Pieces (*Student Guide* Pages 67–70)
Adding on the Base-Ten Board (*Discovery Assignment Book* Pages 103–104)

Daily Practice and Problems and Home Practice
DPP items G–L (*Unit Resource Guide* Pages 18–20)
Home Practice Part 2 (*Discovery Assignment Book* Page 100)

Note: Classrooms whose pacing differs significantly from the suggested pacing of the units should use the Math Facts Calendar in Section 4 of the *Facts Resource Guide* to ensure students receive the complete math facts program.

Assessment Tools
Observational Assessment Record (*Unit Resource Guide* Pages 13–14)

Suggestions for using the DPPs are on page 49.

G. Bit: Change (URG p. 18)

Jade bought a box of juice for 39¢. She paid with a $1 bill. How much change did she get?

What coins could she receive in change? Can you find more than one solution?

J. Challenge: Bicycle Riding (URG p. 19)

James likes to ride his bicycle. He rides two miles every day after school. He rides five miles each weekend day.

1. How far does he ride in one week?
2. How long will it take James to ride 100 miles?

H. Challenge: Cold Cafe (URG p. 19)

The Cold Cafe is an ice cream parlor. The Cafe has three kinds of cones: plain, sugar, and waffle. There are four flavors of ice cream: chocolate, vanilla, strawberry, and mint. How many different one-scoop cones can you get?

K. Bit: Counting Backwards (URG p. 19)

1. Count backwards from 20 to 0 by ones.
2. Count backwards from 100 to 0 by tens.
3. Count backwards from 200 to 100 by tens.

I. Bit: Late for School (URG p. 19)

Lem is always late for school. It takes him 20 minutes to walk to school. If school starts at 8:15 A.M., what time should he leave to be on time?

L. Task: More Bicycle Riding (URG p. 20)

Elly rides her bicycle 4 miles every day. How many days will it take her to ride 100 miles? How many weeks?

Part 1 Addition with Base-Ten Pieces

Review the base-ten pieces, the names of the pieces (bits, skinnies, flats, and packs), and base-ten shorthand. Ask students to explain how the *Base-Ten Board* works (bits live in the bits column, skinnies in the skinnies column, etc.). Ask them about the relationships between the pieces (1 skinny is made up of ten bits, etc.). Then remind them of the imaginary TIMS Candy Company that uses these pieces to keep track of its Chocos—the chocolates the company produces.

As a warm-up, ask students to model the following problem using base-ten pieces and *Base-Ten Boards*.

- *One day Kris made 43 Chocos at the TIMS Candy Company while Andy made 35. How many Chocos did they make altogether?*
- *What is the value of 4 in 43?* (40 or 4 tens)
- *Which pieces represent the 4?* (4 skinnies)
- *What is the value of the 8 in the answer?* (8 or 8 ones)
- *Which pieces represent the 8?* (8 bits)

It is important for children to have established links between the blocks, the shorthand, the symbols, and the words that describe the blocks. As needed, provide more two-digit addition problems that require no regrouping. When appropriate, give students three-digit addition problems—some with one regrouping and some without regrouping. Examples are shown in Figure 3. Students should solve the problems using base-ten pieces and their *Base-Ten Boards*.

Problems without Regrouping	Problems with One Regrouping

Problems without Regrouping

Kris made 214 Chocos while Andy made 143. How many did they make altogether?

```
  2 3 2        3 0 2
+ 1 2 4      + 2 3 5


  2 1 0        1 3 2
+ 1 0 3        2 1 4
             + 5 4 3
```

Problems with One Regrouping

Kris made 148 Chocos while Andy made 236. How many Chocos were made?

```
  1 3 2        5 5 8
+ 2 4 9      + 3 2 6


  3 6 3        1 0 9
+ 2 5 4      + 3 1 1
```

Figure 3: *Three-digit addition*

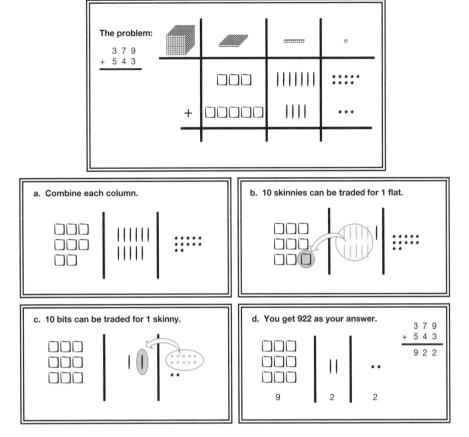

Figure 4: *379 + 543 on the* Base-Ten Board *and recording sheet*

The following sample involves regrouping in two places.

- *Kris made 379 Chocos and Andy made 543. How many Chocos were made altogether?*

Discuss different ways of regrouping. One common way of regrouping is shown in Figure 4. Students may develop other methods that work well for them, including regrouping from the right.

Ask students to discuss Nikia and Maruta's procedure using *Questions 1–5* on the *Adding with Base-Ten Pieces* Activity Pages in the *Student Guide*. Challenge students to complete other problems that involve multiple regroupings. Some examples are shown in Figure 5. Note that the last problem in the figure involves regrouping 10 flats to make a pack.

$$
\begin{array}{r} 438 \\ + \ 374 \end{array} \qquad \begin{array}{r} 489 \\ + \ \ 42 \end{array} \qquad \begin{array}{r} 694 \\ + \ 423 \end{array}
$$

Figure 5: *Three-digit addition with multiple regroupings*

Your students may need to do additional problems together, in groups, or individually. The problems listed in this lesson are meant as a guide. Decide when your class is ready to move on.

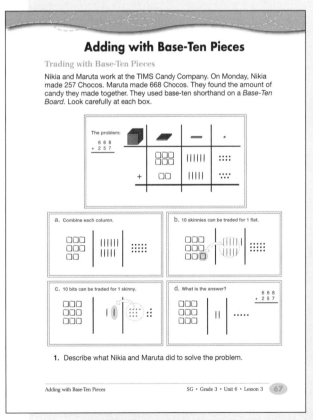

Student Guide - page 67 (Answers on p. 54)

Student Guide Material

2. Nikia started to record her work with the pieces. Copy her work on a *Base-Ten Recording Sheet*. Use the Fewest Pieces Rule. Show how 8 flats, 11 skinnies, and 15 bits will match Nikia and Maruta's answer.

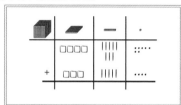

After work on Tuesday, Nikia and Maruta wanted to find out how many Chocos they made together. Nikia made more Chocos than Maruta this time. They set up the problem like this:

3. How many Chocos did Nikia make?

4. How many did Maruta make?

5. Use base-ten pieces and a *Base-Ten Board*. Find the total amount of Chocos Maruta and Nikia made on Tuesday.

Student Guide - page 68 *(Answers on p. 54)*

Name _____ Date _____

Adding on the Base-Ten Board

1. Nikia and Maruta both work at the TIMS Candy Company. Nikia made 136 Chocos. Maruta made 232 Chocos. How much candy did they make together? Solve the problem in two ways. Use base-ten shorthand and use numbers. Use base-ten pieces to help you.

2. Another time Nikia made 237 Chocos and Maruta made 155. Find how much they made altogether. Solve the problem using base-ten shorthand and then with numbers. Make sure you use the Fewest Pieces Rule.

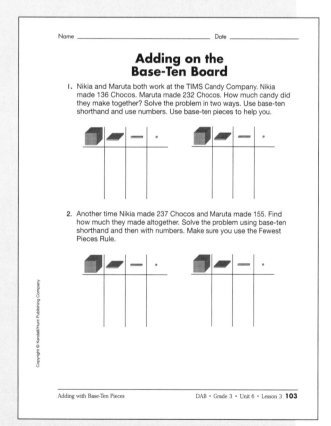

Discovery Assignment Book - page 103 *(Answers on pp. 57–58)*

Figure 6 includes more challenging problems for addition with base-ten pieces. You may choose to delay the introduction of these problems. Remind students there are often several ways to do a problem. Ask them for alternative ways to find answers to the last problem in the figure. Can they do it in their heads? One strategy is to add 2000 to the 3271 and then add on the 6.

$$
\begin{array}{r} 1432 \\ +\ 2085 \end{array} \qquad \begin{array}{r} 2457 \\ +\ 1629 \end{array}
$$

$$
\begin{array}{r} 3109 \\ +\ 928 \end{array} \qquad \begin{array}{r} 2006 \\ +\ 3271 \end{array}
$$

Figure 6: *Four-digit addition with multiple regroupings*

Ask students to complete *Questions 1–2* on the *Adding on the Base-Ten Board* Activity Pages in the *Discovery Assignment Book* in class. You can assign *Questions 3–6* as homework.

Part 2 An Addition Algorithm

This section focuses on further development of the addition algorithm students used in Unit 4. The amount of time you spend on this depends on students' experiences. Be cautious, however, of those who learned the algorithm by rote and do not understand what is behind it. As an informal assessment, ask:

• *Explain how using the algorithm and working with base-ten pieces are similar.*

• *Explain how you use marks to show regrouping.*

If your class is proficient with the addition algorithm, move quickly through this lesson.

Sketch the recording sheets shown in Figure 7 on the board. Ask students when the digits on the recording sheet are the same as the written number—in other words, when the columns are not necessary.

They should realize that the columns can be eliminated when the **Fewest Pieces Rule** is observed. That is, only one digit is allowed in each column of the answer. For example, if there are 3 flats, 14 skinnies, and 4 bits, we cannot eliminate the columns; if we did, the number would then look like 3144. By regrouping this amount, we have 4 flats, 4 skinnies, and 4 bits, which is written as 444.

Remind students that when they solved addition problems with base-ten pieces and recorded their work on the recording sheet, they were, in essence, doing the problems twice. Usually when people add

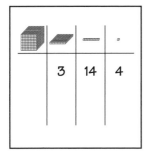
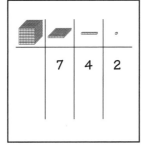
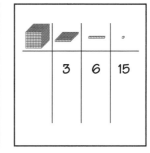

| 3 | 14 | 4 | | 7 | 4 | 2 | | 3 | 6 | 15 |

Figure 7: *Which recording sheet uses the Fewest Pieces Rule?*

they do not use base-ten pieces but a shortcut method based on the recording sheet. The shortcut eliminates the columns. The Fewest Pieces Rule is observed at all times. Show children several examples comparing the recording sheet with the pencil-and-paper algorithm.

In the problem 24 + 38 in Figure 8, we add 4 bits and 8 bits to get 12 bits. Since there are no columns, we cannot write "12." We must regroup in our heads. When regrouping, we have 1 skinny and 2 bits. We record the 2 in the bits column. To keep track of the new skinny, place a 1 above the skinnies' column to remember that there is a new skinny. The total number of skinnies is 6, so the sum is 62.

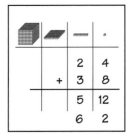

$$\begin{array}{r} \overset{1}{2}\;4 \\ +\;3\;8 \\ \hline 6\;2 \end{array}$$

Figure 8: *Recording the regrouping*

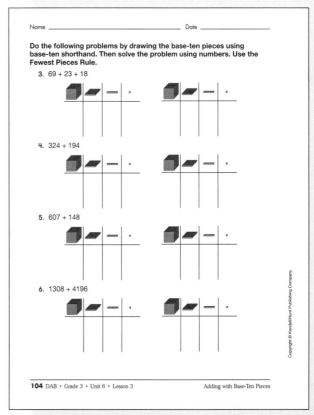

Name _____ Date _____

Do the following problems by drawing the base-ten pieces using base-ten shorthand. Then solve the problem using numbers. Use the Fewest Pieces Rule.

3. 69 + 23 + 18

4. 324 + 194

5. 607 + 148

6. 1308 + 4196

104 DAB · Grade 3 · Unit 6 · Lesson 3   Adding with Base-Ten Pieces

Discovery Assignment Book - page 104 *(Answers on pp. 57–60)*

There are other ways and places to mark "carries" when using a shortcut method. Though the placement of carry marks can vary, it is important to assess whether students understand the reasons for carrying and the value of the carry marks.

Challenge students to solve addition problems that involve more than one regrouping, such as the problem in Figure 9.

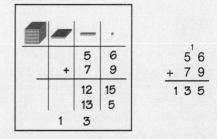

$$\begin{array}{r} \overset{1}{5}\;6 \\ +\;7\;9 \\ \hline 1\;3\;5 \end{array}$$

Figure 9: *Regrouping more than once*

Provide problems where the ones column adds up to more than 20 as shown in Figure 10. Here, 2 skinnies are made from the bits, so write a 2 above the skinnies column.

$$
\begin{array}{r}
\overset{2}{} \\
3\ 6 \\
2\ 9 \\
+\ 3\ 8 \\
\hline
1\ 0\ 3
\end{array}
$$

Figure 10: *Carrying 20*

Use your professional judgment to determine the amount of practice necessary in class and at home. It is best to let the algorithm sink in slowly. Assigning a few problems a day over a long period of time is better than assigning many at once and expecting immediate fluency.

Give students problems involving three- and four-digit addends. Figure 11 shows some examples. Ask students to complete *Questions 6–9* in the *Student Guide.*

$$
\begin{array}{r} 2\ 3\ 4\ 6 \\ +\ 1\ 0\ 7\ 7 \end{array}
\qquad
\begin{array}{r} 7\ 6\ 5 \\ +\ \ \ \ 8\ 9 \end{array}
\qquad
\begin{array}{r} 2\ 3\ 0\ 5 \\ +\ 3\ 7\ 0\ 6 \end{array}
$$

Figure 11: *Multidigit addition*

More Shortcut Addition

Kris has worked at the TIMS Candy Company for a long time. Kris knows that it is not necessary to use the record sheet when adding. He can use the Fewest Pieces Rule and write only 1 digit in each column.

He showed his shortcut method to Andy.

$$
\begin{array}{r} \overset{1}{5}4 \\ +\ 47 \\ \hline 101 \end{array}
$$

6. Why did Kris put the 1 above the 5? What does the 1 mean?

Andy tried a problem, too.

$$
\begin{array}{r} 647 \\ +\ 285 \\ \hline 932 \end{array}
$$

7. Why did Andy put a 1 above the 4? What does the 1 mean?

8. Why did Andy put a 1 above the 6? What does that 1 mean?

Now try this problem:

$$
\begin{array}{r} 435 \\ +\ 168 \end{array}
$$

Katie, Scott, and Nora solved the problem using paper and pencil. Here is their work.

Katie's solution	Scott's solution	Nora's solution
$\begin{array}{r}\overset{11}{4}35\\+\ 168\\\hline 603\end{array}$	$\begin{array}{r}435\\+\ 168\\\hline 603\end{array}$	$\begin{array}{r}435\\+\ 168\\\hline 13\\90\\500\\\hline 603\end{array}$

9. Compare the three pencil-and-paper solutions. Explain what Katie, Scott, and Nora did to find their answers.

***Student Guide - page 69** (Answers on p. 55)*

Content Note

Some students may need or prefer to continue using base-ten pieces longer than others. It is also not unusual for a student to sporadically return to the use of manipulatives. Sometimes, when a child becomes confused using a paper-and-pencil algorithm it can suffice to say, "Think of the base-ten pieces." Using base-ten shorthand also should help in developing images of the pieces.

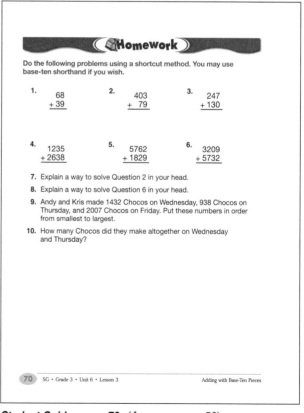

Homework

Do the following problems using a shortcut method. You may use base-ten shorthand if you wish.

1. $\begin{array}{r}68\\+\ 39\end{array}$ **2.** $\begin{array}{r}403\\+\ 79\end{array}$ **3.** $\begin{array}{r}247\\+\ 130\end{array}$

4. $\begin{array}{r}1235\\+\ 2638\end{array}$ **5.** $\begin{array}{r}5762\\+\ 1829\end{array}$ **6.** $\begin{array}{r}3209\\+\ 5732\end{array}$

7. Explain a way to solve Question 2 in your head.

8. Explain a way to solve Question 6 in your head.

9. Andy and Kris made 1432 Chocos on Wednesday, 938 Chocos on Thursday, and 2007 Chocos on Friday. Put these numbers in order from smallest to largest.

10. How many Chocos did they make altogether on Wednesday and Thursday?

***Student Guide - page 70** (Answers on p. 56)*

Math Facts

DPP Challenge H is a word problem that provides practice with multiplication facts.

Homework and Practice

- You can assign *Questions 3–6* on the *Adding on the Base-Ten Board* Activity Pages in the *Discovery Assignment Book* as homework at the end of Part 1.

- Assign *Questions 1–10* in the Homework section in the *Student Guide* after Part 2.

- Assign Part 2 of the Home Practice in the *Discovery Assignment Book* as homework as it provides extra practice with addition and subtraction.

- Suggest that when doing the addition and subtraction problems at home students and parents work with pennies, dimes, and dollars (pieces of paper can be substituted for 1 dollar and 10 dollar bills). Just as 10 bits are traded for a skinny, 10 pennies are traded for a dime, etc. You can pretend the problems are stated in pennies. Children benefit from working in another context.

- DPP items G, J, and L are multistep word problems that provide computation practice. Item G involves money. Bit I is a problem involving elapsed time, and Bit K builds number sense by skip counting backwards.

Answers for Part 2 of the Home Practice are in the Answer Key at the end of this lesson and at the end of this unit.

Assessment

Informally assess your students' understanding by asking groups to explain their work as they solve problems using base-ten pieces. If the opportunity arises, show the class a method devised by a student. Ask the other children to explain the method and determine its validity. Record your observations on the *Observational Assessment Record*.

Name _____ Date _____

Unit 6 Home Practice

PART 1

1. A. 15 − 9 = _____   B. 17 − 10 = _____
   C. 9 − 4 = _____   D. 11 − 7 = _____
   E. 7 − 2 = _____   F. 12 − 3 = _____
   G. 14 − 8 = _____   H. 18 − 9 = _____

2. Leah has a hard time finding the answer to 1G. How did you find the answer to this subtraction fact? Share your method.

PART 2

1. Solve the addition and subtraction problems. Show how you solved each one.
   A. 156 + 54 = _____   B. 232 − 29 = _____

2. Sharon works at a flower shop. She received a shipment of roses and carnations. She received 48 roses. She received 60 more carnations than roses. Show how you solved the following problems.

   A. How many carnations did she receive? _____

   B. How many flowers did she receive in all? _____

100 DAB · Grade 3 · Unit 6   MORE ADDING AND SUBTRACTING

Discovery Assignment Book - page 100 (Answers on p. 56)

At a Glance

Math Facts and Daily Practice and Problems

DPP Challenge H provides practice with multiplication facts. Items G, J, and L provide computation practice. Item I involves time, and item K builds number sense.

Part 1. Addition with Base-Ten Pieces

1. Review base-ten pieces and shorthand.
2. Provide addition problems with and without regrouping.
3. Students complete *Questions 1–5* in the *Student Guide.*
4. Students complete the *Adding on the Base-Ten Board* Activity Pages in the *Discovery Assignment Book.*

Part 2. An Addition Algorithm

1. Discuss that students can eliminate columns on recording sheets when the Fewest Pieces Rule is observed.
2. Review and extend the standard addition algorithm as a shortcut for adding three- and four-digit numbers.
3. Students complete *Questions 6–9* in the *Student Guide.*

Homework

1. Assign *Questions 3–6* on the *Adding on the Base-Ten Board* Activity Pages in the *Discovery Assignment Book* after Part 1.
2. Assign the Homework section in the *Student Guide* after Part 2.
3. You can assign Part 2 of the Home Practice for more practice with addition and subtraction.

Assessment

Use the *Observational Assessment Record* to note students' progress representing addition using base-ten pieces.

Answer Key is on pages 54–60.

Notes:

Base-Ten Board Part 1

Skinnies

Bits

Base-Ten Board Part 2

Flats

Packs

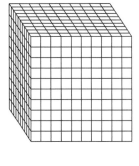

Blackline Master

Base-Ten Recording Sheet

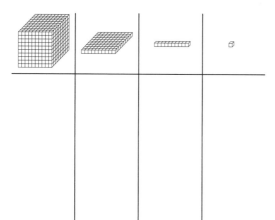

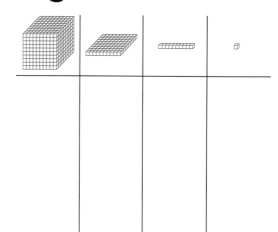

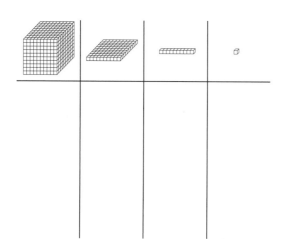

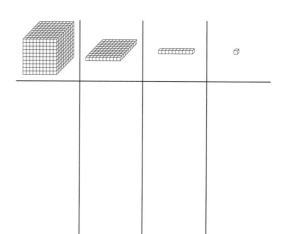

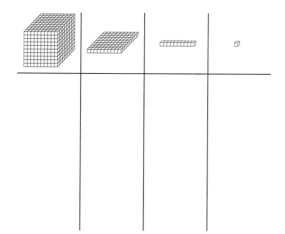

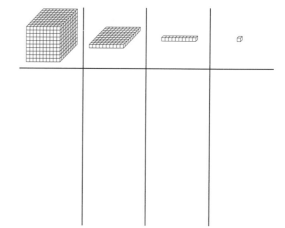

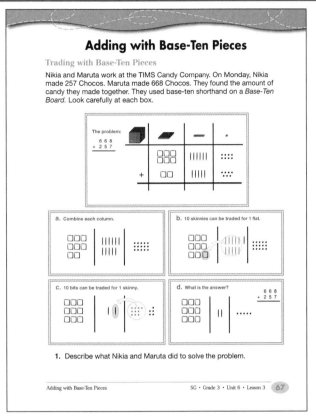

Student Guide - page 67

Student Guide (p. 67)

1. Explanations will vary. First they combined all the pieces in each column. They had 8 flats, 11 skinnies, and 15 bits. This answer does not satisfy the Fewest Pieces Rule. They traded 10 skinnies for 1 flat and then had 9 flats altogether. They only had 1 skinny after the trade. After trading 10 bits for 1 skinny, they had 2 skinnies. Altogether they had 9 flats, 2 skinnies, and 5 bits. Their answer is 925.

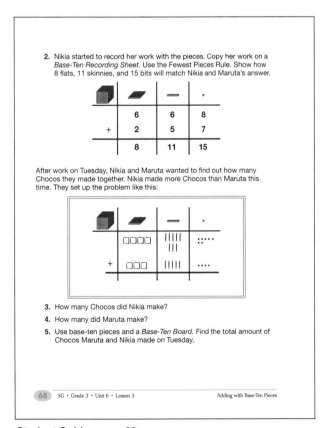

Student Guide - page 68

Student Guide (p. 68)

2.

	6	6	8
+	2	5	7
	8	11	15
	8	12	5
	9	2	5

3. 487 Chocos

4. 354 Chocos

5. 841 Chocos; methods will vary. Students can trade 10 skinnies for 1 flat. This gives them 8 flats altogether; 10 bits can be traded for 1 skinny. This gives them 4 skinnies altogether. One bit remains.

Student Guide (p. 69)

6. Kris had 11 bits. He traded 10 for 1 skinny. The 1 above the 5 shows the new skinny.

7. Andy had 12 bits. He traded 10 bits for 1 skinny. The 1 above the 4 shows the new skinny.

8. Andy had 13 skinnies. He traded 10 skinnies for 1 flat. The 1 above the 6 shows the new flat.

9. Explanations will vary.

Katie's solution: Katie started with 13 bits. She traded 10 of them for 1 skinny. The 1 above the 3 shows the new skinny. Then she added the total number of skinnies. She had 10 skinnies. She traded all 10 skinnies for 1 flat. There were no skinnies left so she recorded a 0 in the skinnies column. The new flat was recorded by writing a 1 above the 4. She added all the flats; she had 6.

Scott's solution: Scott's method of trading is similar to Katie's. He recorded the new skinny and flat with 1s as well. However, he recorded them at the bottom of the flat and skinny columns instead of at the top.

Nora's solution: Nora had 13 bits to start with. She traded 10 bits for 1 skinny and recorded 13. She added 3 skinnies and 6 skinnies and got 9 skinnies. She recorded this in a new row as 90, 9 skinnies and 0 bits. She added 4 flats and 1 flat and got 5 flats. In a third row she recorded 500 or 5 flats, 0 skinnies, and 0 bits. Altogether she had 5 flats, 10 skinnies, and 3 bits. The little 1 shows that she traded the 10 skinnies for 1 flat. No skinnies remained.

More Shortcut Addition

Kris has worked at the TIMS Candy Company for a long time. Kris knows that it is not necessary to use the record sheet when adding. He can use the Fewest Pieces Rule and write only 1 digit in each column.

He showed his shortcut method to Andy.

$$\begin{array}{r} 54 \\ + 47 \\ \hline 101 \end{array}$$

6. Why did Kris put the 1 above the 5? What does the 1 mean?

Andy tried a problem, too.

$$\begin{array}{r} 647 \\ + 285 \\ \hline 932 \end{array}$$

7. Why did Andy put a 1 above the 4? What does the 1 mean?

8. Why did Andy put a 1 above the 6? What does that 1 mean?

Now try this problem:

$$\begin{array}{r} 435 \\ + 168 \end{array}$$

Katie, Scott, and Nora solved the problem using paper and pencil. Here is their work.

Katie's solution	Scott's solution	Nora's solution
$\begin{array}{r} 435 \\ + 168 \\ \hline 603 \end{array}$	$\begin{array}{r} 435 \\ + 168 \\ \hline 603 \end{array}$	$\begin{array}{r} 435 \\ + 168 \\ \hline 13 \\ 90 \\ 500 \\ \hline 603 \end{array}$

9. Compare the three pencil-and-paper solutions. Explain what Katie, Scott, and Nora did to find their answers.

Student Guide - page 69

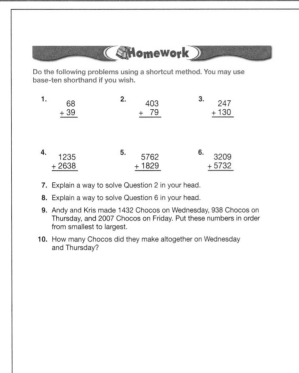

Student Guide - page 70

Student Guide (p. 70)

Homework

Solution strategies will vary.

1. 107

2. 482

3. 377

4. 3873

5. 7591

6. 8941

7. Possible strategy:
   $79 + 1 = 80$;
   $402 + 80 = 482$

8. Possible strategy:
   $32 + 9 = 41$;
   $3200 + 5700 = 8900$;
   $8900 + 41 = 8941$

9. 938, 1432, 2007

10. 2370 Chocos

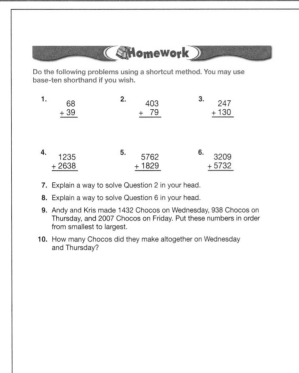

Discovery Assignment Book - page 100

Discovery Assignment Book (p. 100)

Home Practice*

Part 2

Questions 1–2

1. **A.** 210 ($56 + 54 = 110, 110 + 100 = 210$)
   Strategies will vary.

   B. 203 ($32 - 29 = 3, 3 + 200 = 203$)
   Strategies will vary.

2. **A.** 108 carnations ($48 + 60 = 108$)
   Strategies will vary.

   B. 156 flowers ($108 + 48 = 156$)
   Strategies will vary.

*Answers for all the Home Practice in the *Discovery Assignment Book* are at the end of the unit.

Discovery Assignment Book (pp. 103–104)

Adding on the Base-Ten Board

Ways of recording solutions on the base-ten board will vary. One possible solution strategy for each problem is shown on pages 58–60.

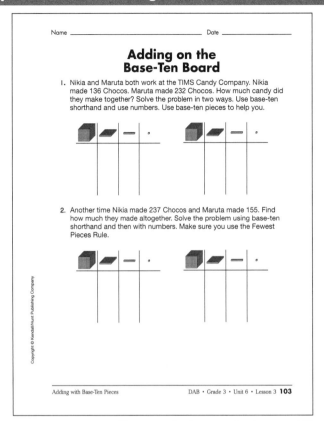

Name _____ Date _____

Adding on the Base-Ten Board

1. Nikia and Maruta both work at the TIMS Candy Company. Nikia made 136 Chocos. Maruta made 232 Chocos. How much candy did they make together? Solve the problem in two ways. Use base-ten shorthand and use numbers. Use base-ten pieces to help you.

2. Another time Nikia made 237 Chocos and Maruta made 155. Find how much they made altogether. Solve the problem using base-ten shorthand and then with numbers. Make sure you use the Fewest Pieces Rule.

Adding with Base-Ten Pieces   DAB • Grade 3 • Unit 6 • Lesson 3 **103**

Discovery Assignment Book - page 103

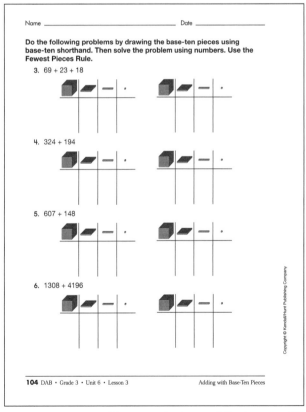

Name _____ Date _____

Do the following problems by drawing the base-ten pieces using base-ten shorthand. Then solve the problem using numbers. Use the Fewest Pieces Rule.

3. 69 + 23 + 18

4. 324 + 194

5. 607 + 148

6. 1308 + 4196

104 DAB • Grade 3 • Unit 6 • Lesson 3   Adding with Base-Ten Pieces

Discovery Assignment Book - page 104

1.

2.

3.

4.

5.

	6	0	7
+	1	4	8
	7	4¹	1̶5̶ ⁵
	7	5	5

6.

1	3	0	8
+ 4	1	9	6
5	4	9¹	1̶4̶ ⁴
5	4¹	1̶0̶ ⁰	4
5	5	0	4

Lesson 4

Subtracting with Base-Ten Pieces

Estimated Class Sessions

4

Lesson Overview

Students explore subtraction in this lesson. In Part 1 students subtract using base-ten pieces, *Base-Ten Boards,* and *Base-Ten Recording Sheets.* In Part 2 a standard subtraction algorithm is introduced as a shortcut to working with the recording sheets.

Key Content

- Understanding place value.
- Representing subtraction using base-ten pieces.
- Developing a subtraction algorithm.
- Subtracting using paper and pencil.

Homework

1. Assign the Homework section of the *Subtracting on the Base-Ten Board* Activity Pages in the *Discovery Assignment Book* after Part 1.
2. Assign the Homework section in the *Student Guide* after Part 2.

Assessment

1. Use *Questions 6-14* in the *Student Guide* to assess students' abilities to solve problems involving addition and subtraction. You can score *Question 10* using the Knowing dimension of the *TIMS Multidimensional Rubric.*
2. Use the Homework section in the *Discovery Assignment Book* and the *Observational Assessment Record* to note students' progress subtracting using base-ten pieces and paper and pencil.
3. Use DPP Task R as a short assessment.

Materials List

Supplies and Copies

Student	Teacher
Supplies for Each Student Pair or Group of Three	**Supplies**
• 1 set of base-ten pieces: 2 packs, 14 flats, 30 skinnies, and 50 bits	
Copies	**Copies/Transparencies**
• 1 copy of *Base-Ten Board* per student pair (*Unit Resource Guide* Pages 51–52)	• 1 transparency of *Base-Ten Board,* optional (*Unit Resource Guide* Pages 51–52)
• 1 copy of *Base-Ten Recording Sheet* per student (*Unit Resource Guide* Page 53)	• 1 transparency of *Base-Ten Recording Sheet,* optional (*Unit Resource Guide* Page 53)

All blackline masters including assessment, transparency, and DPP masters are also on the Teacher Resource CD.

Student Books

Subtracting with Base-Ten Pieces (*Student Guide* Pages 71–76)
Student Rubric: *Knowing* (*Student Guide* Appendix A and Inside Back Cover)
Subtracting on the Base-Ten Board (*Discovery Assignment Book* Pages 105–108)

Daily Practice and Problems and Home Practice

DPP items M–T (*Unit Resource Guide* Pages 20–22)

Note: Classrooms whose pacing differs significantly from the suggested pacing of the units should use the Math Facts Calendar in Section 4 of the *Facts Resource Guide* to ensure students receive the complete math facts program.

Assessment Tools

Observational Assessment Record (*Unit Resource Guide* Pages 13–14)
TIMS Multidimensional Rubric (*Teacher Implementation Guide,* Assessment section)

Daily Practice and Problems

Suggestions for using the DPPs are on page 71.

M. Bit: Calculator Counting Starting at 5 (URG p. 20)

Use your calculator to count.

A. Start at 5 and count by 10s to 200. Press 5 + 10 = = = = . . . Count quietly to yourself. Describe any patterns you see. Can you stop exactly on 200?

B. Start at 5 and count by 9s to 200. Press 5 + 9 = = = = . . . Count quietly to yourself. Describe any patterns you see. Can you stop exactly on 200?

N. Task: Adding Nine (URG p. 20)

Write the following problems on a piece of paper, then solve them. Look for patterns.

1. 14 + 9 =   2. 104 + 9 =
3. 41 + 9 =   4. 23 + 9 =
5. 32 + 9 =   6. 42 + 9 =
7. 77 + 9 =   8. 68 + 9 =
9. 95 + 9 =

O. Bit: Past, Present, and Future (URG p. 21)

What is the date today?

What will the date be in 9 days?

What was the date 9 days ago?

P. Challenge: Change for $1 (URG p. 21)

How many ways can you make change for $1 using only nickels and dimes? Prove your answer.

Q. Bit: Past, Present, and Future Again (URG p. 21)

What is the day of the week today?

What day will it be in 9 days?

What day was it 9 days ago?

How did you find your answers?

R. Task: Inventions (URG p. 22)

1. The first zipper was invented in 1893. About how many years ago was the zipper invented? Exactly how many years?

2. The first wooden pencils were square. They were invented in 1683. Rounded pencils were invented in 1876. How long did people use square pencils before round ones were invented? Is your answer reasonable?

S. Bit: Basketball Points (URG p. 22)

In 1962, Wilt Chamberlain scored a total of 4029 points in games. In 1970, Jerry West scored 2309 points. In 1992, Michael Jordan scored 2404 points. Put the number of total points for these players in order from smallest to largest. You can use base-ten pieces to help you.

T. Task: Time (URG p. 22)

1. How many minutes are in $1\frac{1}{2}$ hours?
2. It takes Karen $\frac{1}{2}$ hour to wash the dishes. If she washes dishes every night for a week, how many minutes will she spend washing the dishes? How many hours?

Part 1 **Subtraction with Base-Ten Pieces**

Explain that students will again assist the workers at the TIMS Candy Company. The company owns a store next to the factory where they sell their Chocos. Workers keep track of the store's inventory—the amount of candy in the store—with base-ten pieces. Challenge students with the following problem.

- *At the beginning of the day, there were 57 Chocos. Customers bought 32. How many are left?*

Ask students to model the problem with base-ten pieces and to record their work on the *Base-Ten Recording Sheet.* See Figure 12. Note that when modeling with base-ten pieces, we show the second quantity (32) as being removed from the *Base-Ten Board.*

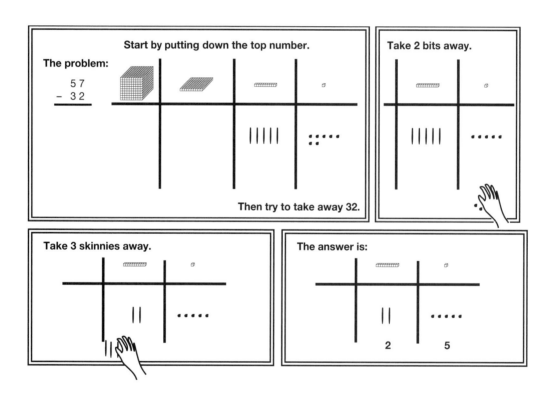

Figure 12: *57 – 32 on the Base-Ten Board*

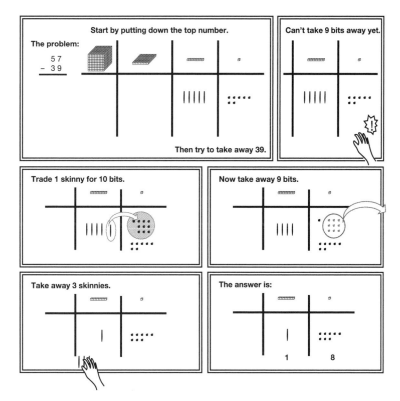

Figure 13: *57 − 39 on the Base-Ten Board*

Provide more problems that do not involve regrouping.

Students can then begin exploring problems that involve regrouping. For example:

• *On another day, there were 57 Chocos, but customers bought 39. How many were left?*

Students should begin by representing 57 Chocos with base-ten pieces. They will realize that 9 bits cannot be removed because there are only 7. Ask:

• *Can you somehow take the 9 bits away?*

If students do not suggest exchanging 1 skinny for 10 bits, demonstrate the trade. Students are left with one less skinny and 17 bits. This problem is shown in Figure 13.

Provide several more problems that involve regrouping once, such as the sample problems in Figure 14.

$$
\begin{array}{r} 73 \\ -\ 28 \end{array}
\qquad
\begin{array}{r} 45 \\ -\ 16 \end{array}
\qquad
\begin{array}{r} 90 \\ -\ 56 \end{array}
$$

$$
\begin{array}{r} 283 \\ -\ 146 \end{array}
\qquad
\begin{array}{r} 417 \\ -\ 42 \end{array}
\qquad
\begin{array}{r} 517 \\ -\ 235 \end{array}
$$

Figure 14: *Subtraction problems with one regrouping*

Informally assess students' understanding by asking them to explain the values of certain base-ten pieces. Also, ask them to explain and model their regrouping.

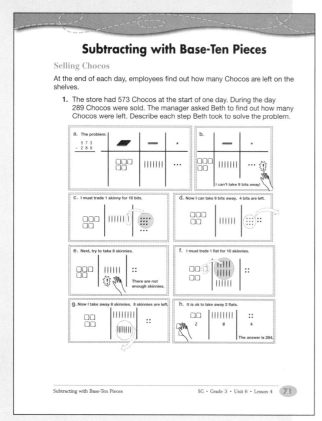

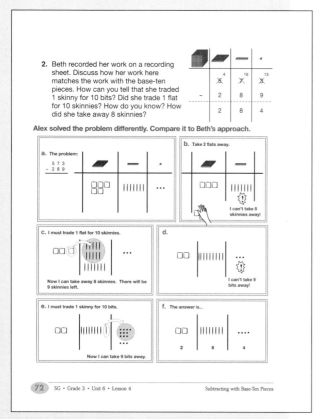

Provide problems that involve regrouping in more than one column. For example:

- *The store began the day with 563 Chocos. During the day, 265 Chocos were sold. How many were left?*

Model the regrouping process. Instruct students to model the problem with base-ten pieces and record their work on the recording sheet. Figure 15 demonstrates one way of regrouping. However, some students may begin the problem from the left, use different strategies, or record the trades in different ways. Discuss various approaches and which methods are more efficient. Some students may find it easier to do all the regroupings at once and then subtract.

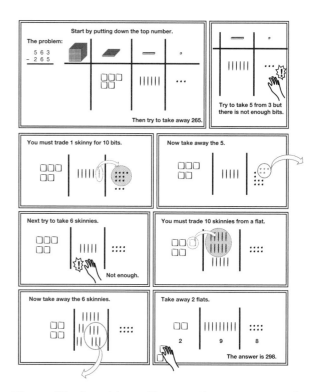

Figure 15: *A problem with more than one regrouping*

Questions 1–3 on the *Subtracting with Base-Ten Pieces* Activity Pages in the *Student Guide* will help review key concepts in subtracting with base-ten pieces and recording sheets. Ask students to compare different methods.

Provide problems that involve a middle zero such as 105 − 76. Instruct students to represent 105 using the fewest pieces. In this case, students cannot subtract 6 bits from 5 bits. Ask:

- *How many skinnies are there?* (none)
- *How many skinnies are in the 1 flat?* (10)

- *Regroup 1 flat into 10 skinnies and then 1 skinny into 10 bits. How many bits are there altogether?* (15)
- *If I take away 6 bits, how many are left?* (9)

Figure 16 shows one way this problem can be recorded. Walk students through each step of recording this problem.

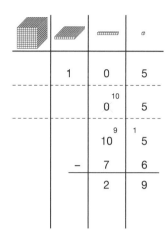

Figure 16: *105 – 76*

Encourage students to solve the problem a second way as a check. For example, students may think $105 - 75 = 30$, so $105 - 76$ is one less or 29. Another strategy is to count up.

$76 + ④ = 80$

$80 + ⑳ = 100$

$100 + ⑤ = 105$

$4 + 20 + 5 = 29$

Figure 17 shows more subtraction problems to solve with the whole class, in groups, or individually. The amount of guidance and practice needed will depend on students' experience. Do not expect mastery immediately. Requiring children to do too many of these problems may result in boredom and frustration. It is best to assign a few problems a day over a longer period of time.

```
   367        1623        407       3000
 - 123       - 828       - 69      - 524
```

Figure 17: *A variety of subtraction problems*

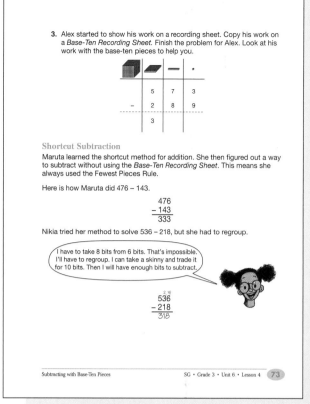

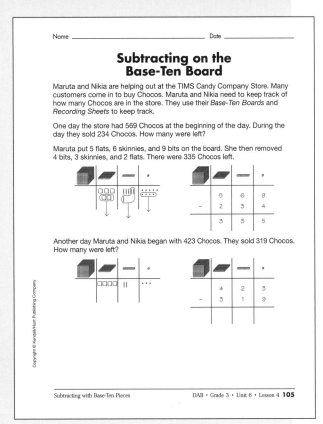

Discovery Assignment Book - page 105

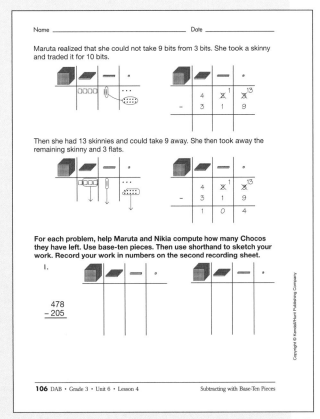

Discovery Assignment Book - page 106 (Answers on p. 76)

Note that the last three problems involve regrouping several times. Students often have trouble with problems such as the last one. Point out that they can do the problems by alternative methods. Ask children to suggest some different strategies. For example, they can solve $3000 - 524$ by first doing $2999 - 524$ and then adding 1 to the answer. Using this method, no regrouping is required; they also can do $3000 - 524$ mentally by first subtracting 500 (2500), then subtracting 20 (2480), and finally subtracting 4 (2476).

Ask students to study the examples on the *Subtracting on the Base-Ten Board* Activity Pages in the *Discovery Assignment Book* and complete *Questions 1–4*.

Part 2 A Subtraction Algorithm

After students have had sufficient practice solving subtraction problems using base-ten pieces, introduce them to the idea that, just as there are shortcut ways to add, there are shortcut ways to subtract. One method relies on using the Fewest Pieces Rule. Only one digit is allowed in each column of the answer, so column markings are not necessary.

Provide problems that do not involve regrouping, such as $48 - 23$. Ask students to compare the work done on a recording sheet with the shortcut way of subtracting shown in Figure 18.

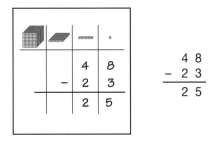

Figure 18: *Comparing a recording sheet with the shortcut method*

Next, introduce problems that involve regrouping, such as 74 − 38. Note to the class that since we cannot take 8 bits from 4 bits, we must regroup. We break up one of the skinnies to make 14 bits. To remember this, write a 14 above the bits column. We also cross out the 7 and write 6 above because now there are only 6 skinnies. See Figure 19. As you discuss the algorithm, incorporate questions that will check students' understanding of regrouping.

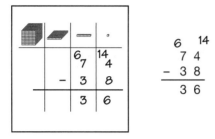

Figure 19: *Breaking up skinnies*

Provide several problems such as those in Figure 20. Ask student groups to solve them. As they work the problems, walk around and ask questions about the value of certain digits and what each of the steps means.

$$
\begin{array}{r} 6\,3 \\ -\,2\,5 \\ \hline \end{array}
\qquad
\begin{array}{r} 9\,2 \\ -\,4\,0 \\ \hline \end{array}
\qquad
\begin{array}{r} 5\,0 \\ -\,1\,9 \\ \hline \end{array}
$$

$$
\begin{array}{r} 1\,8\,6 \\ -\ \ 4\,7 \\ \hline \end{array}
\qquad
\begin{array}{r} 4\,2\,2 \\ -\,1\,7\,0 \\ \hline \end{array}
\qquad
\begin{array}{r} 2\,4\,5\,2 \\ -\,1\,3\,2\,1 \\ \hline \end{array}
$$

$$
\begin{array}{r} 4\,5\,6 \\ -\,1\,0\,9 \\ \hline \end{array}
\qquad
\begin{array}{r} 3\,9\,0 \\ -\ \ 2\,2 \\ \hline \end{array}
\qquad
\begin{array}{r} 2\,3\,4\,5 \\ -\,1\,0\,5\,4 \\ \hline \end{array}
$$

Figure 20: *Subtraction problems with no or one regrouping*

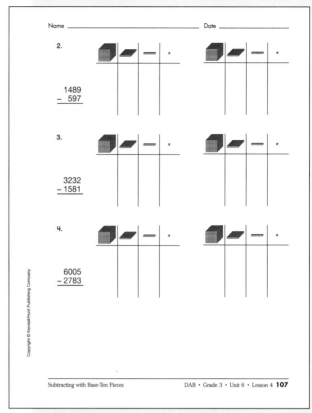

Discovery Assignment Book - page 107 (Answers on pp. 77–78)

4. Explain why Maruta wrote the 4 above the 5 and 16 above the 6 in the problem below.

$$
\begin{array}{r} \overset{4\ 16}{7\,5\,6} \\ -\,1\,6\,7 \\ \hline 9 \end{array}
$$

5. Maruta continued the problem. Explain why she wrote a 6 above the 7 and a 14 above the 4.

$$
\begin{array}{r} \overset{14}{\underset{}{6\ \overset{4\ 16}{\cancel{7}\,5\,6}}} \\ -\,1\,6\,7 \\ \hline 5\,8\,9 \end{array}
$$

Dime Store Problems

Art's Dime Store is a favorite for many third graders. It has almost anything a third grader would want, and the people who work there are friendly to kids.

Art's Dime Store sells LOTS of penny candy (candy that costs only 1¢). The table below shows how much penny candy the store sold in the first four months of the year.

6. How much penny candy did the store sell in January and February together?

7. The store sold lots of candy in February because Valentine's Day is February 14. How much more penny candy did the store sell in February than in January?

8. The biggest month for selling penny candy is October because that's when Halloween is. Art thinks that he will sell as much candy in October as he did in March and April combined. How much candy should Art order for October?

Month	Number of Pieces of Candy Sold
January	2394
February	5620
March	3306
April	4885

74   SG • Grade 3 • Unit 6 • Lesson 4   Subtracting with Base-Ten Pieces

Student Guide - page 74 (Answers on p. 74)

9. Make up and solve two of your own problems about penny candy sales at Art's Dime Store.

10. Art's Dime Store has four large tanks of goldfish. Here are Art's inventory records for the goldfish last week:

Number of goldfish at beginning of week	588
Number of new goldfish Art bought from his supplier	603
Number of goldfish sold to customers	462
Number of goldfish that died	81

At the end of the week, did Art have more or fewer goldfish than he had at the beginning of the week? Explain.

Art has to keep careful records of all his sales. Here are the daily total sales for the store during the first week in April.

Day of the Week Sale	Sales (in dollars)
Monday	5271
Tuesday	3008
Wednesday	3065
Thursday	4753
Friday	4329
Saturday	8297
Sunday	6084

11. The busiest days for the store are usually on the weekend. What were the sales for Saturday and Sunday together?

12. How much more were the combined sales of Saturday and Sunday than the combined sales of the next two busiest days?

13. During the same week last year, the store's sales on Tuesday were $2862. How much more did Art's Dime Store sell this year on Tuesday?

14. Make up and solve your own problems about sales at Art's Dime Store.

Subtracting with Base-Ten Pieces   SG • Grade 3 • Unit 6 • Lesson 4   **75**

Student Guide - page 75 *(Answers on p. 75)*

When students are ready, provide problems, such as those in Figure 21, that involve regrouping more than once. Ask them to estimate the answer before they begin. This will help them decide whether their answer is reasonable. If children have difficulty, suggest they use base-ten pieces. Understanding is far more important than memorizing the procedure.

$$\begin{array}{r} 325 \\ -\,157 \end{array} \qquad \begin{array}{r} 1234 \\ -\,876 \end{array} \qquad \begin{array}{r} 2005 \\ -\,246 \end{array} \qquad \begin{array}{r} 1020 \\ -\,234 \end{array}$$

Figure 21: *Subtraction problems with more than one regrouping*

Encourage students to look for other strategies to solve the problems. For example, students can count up to subtract $2005 - 246$:
$246 + ④ = 250$;
$250 + ⑤⓪ = 300$;
$300 + ⑦⓪⓪ = 1000$;
$1000 + ①⓪⓪⓪ = 2000$;
$2000 + ⑤ = 2005$.
Adding gives
$4 + 50 + 700 + 1000 = 1754$.

Ask students to complete *Questions 4–14* in the *Student Guide*. Students can complete the problems working in groups, individually, or for homework.

Name _____   Date _____

Homework

Solve each problem two ways. First, use base-ten shorthand on the recording sheet. Then use a shortcut method or mental math. Show or explain your method.

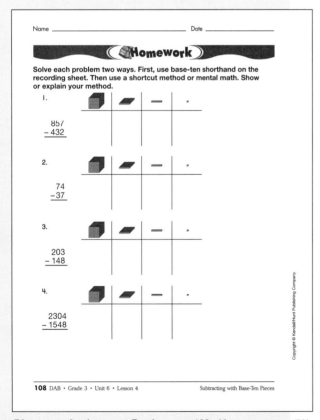

1.

   857
 − 432

2.

   74
 − 37

3.

   203
 − 148

4.

   2304
 − 1548

108 DAB • Grade 3 • Unit 6 • Lesson 4   Subtracting with Base-Ten Pieces

Discovery Assignment Book - page 108 *(Answers on p. 79)*

70   URG • Grade 3 • Unit 6 • Lesson 4

Homework and Practice

- Assign the Homework section of the *Subtracting on the Base-Ten Board* Activity Pages in the *Discovery Assignment Book* after Part 1.

- Assign the Homework section in the *Student Guide* after Part 2.

- DPP items M and N build number sense. Bits O and Q involve calculations on a calendar. Challenge P is a problem about combinations of coins. For Bit S, students compare and order large numbers. Task T provides practice with elapsed time.

Assessment

- Use the Dime Store Problems in *Questions 6–14* in the *Student Guide* to assess students' understanding of addition and subtraction and problem solving. You can assess *Question 10* using the Student Rubric: *Knowing.* Refer students to the rubric.

- Use *Questions 1–4* in the Homework section of the *Discovery Assignment Book* to assess students' progress with subtraction. Record your observations in the *Observational Assessment Record.*

- Use DPP Task R to assess students' abilities to solve problems involving subtraction.

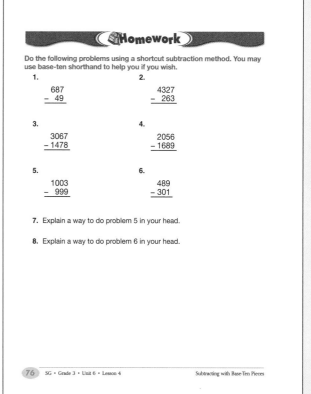

Student Guide - page 76 (Answers on p. 75)

At a Glance

Math Facts and Daily Practice and Problems

DPP items M, N, and S build number sense. Items O and Q involve calculating on a calendar. Item P is a challenging money problem. Item R provides computation practice and item T provides practice with time.

Part 1. Subtraction with Base-Ten Pieces

1. Explain that the TIMS Candy Company has a store where it sells Chocos. The company keeps track of inventory using base-ten pieces.
2. Students use base-ten pieces, *Base-Ten Boards,* and *Base-Ten Recording Sheets* to solve subtraction problems involving regrouping.
3. Students complete *Questions 1–3* in the S*tudent Guide.*
4. Students complete the *Subtracting on the Base-Ten Board* Activity Pages in the *Discovery Assignment Book.*

Part 2. A Subtraction Algorithm

1. Introduce the idea of a shortcut for solving subtraction problems.
2. Students use a subtraction algorithm to solve problems, some requiring regrouping, some not.
3. Students complete and discuss *Questions 4–14* in the *Student Guide.*

Homework

1. Assign the Homework section of the *Subtracting on the Base-Ten Board* Activity Pages in the *Discovery Assignment Book* after Part 1.
2. Assign the Homework section in the *Student Guide* after Part 2.

Assessment

1. Use *Questions 6–14* in the *Student Guide* to assess students' abilities to solve problems involving addition and subtraction. You can score *Question 10* using the Knowing dimension of the *TIMS Multidimensional Rubric.*
2. Use the Homework section in the *Discovery Assignment Book* and the *Observational Assessment Record* to note students' progress with subtracting using base-ten pieces and paper and pencil.
3. Use Task R as a short assessment.

Answer Key is on pages 73–79.

Notes:

Student Guide (p. 71)

Subtracting with Base-Ten Pieces

1. Beth's work on the *Base-Ten Board:*

Explanations will vary. Beth first tried to take 9 bits away but she couldn't because she had only 3 bits. She traded 1 skinny for 10 bits. Now she had 13 bits, so she took away 9, leaving 4 bits. She then tried to take away 8 skinnies. She couldn't because she had only 6 skinnies. She traded one flat for ten skinnies. She now had 16 skinnies and could take away 8, leaving 8. Beth then took away 2 flats, leaving 2. In her three columns, she was left with 2 flats, 8 skinnies, and 4 bits, or 284.

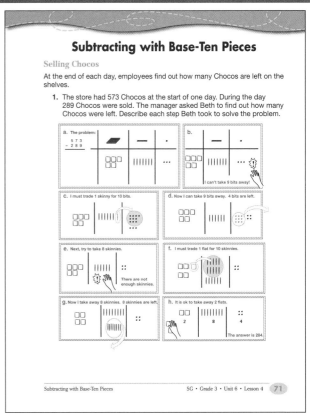

Student Guide - page 71

Student Guide (p. 72)

2. Beth's work on the recording sheet:

Explanations will vary. Beth crossed out the 7 and wrote a 6 to show she traded 1 skinny for 10 bits. She then had 13 bits, so she crossed out the 3 and recorded 13. She could then subtract 9 bits from 13 bits and write 4 below. With only 6 skinnies she couldn't take away 8 skinnies. Beth crossed out the 5 in the flats column and wrote a 4 to show she traded 1 flat for 10 skinnies. The 16 shows she added the 6 skinnies she had to the 10 new ones. She could then subtract 8 skinnies from the 16 skinnies.

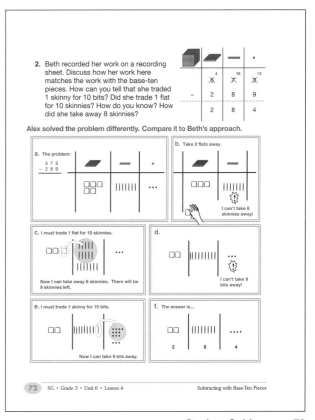

Student Guide - page 72

Student Guide (p. 73)

3. Alex's recording sheet:

<table>
<tr><td>(flat)</td><td>(skinny)</td><td>(bit line)</td><td>(bit)</td></tr>
<tr><td></td><td></td><td>17</td><td>13</td></tr>
<tr><td>5</td><td>7</td><td>7</td><td>3</td></tr>
<tr><td>− 2</td><td>8</td><td>8</td><td>9</td></tr>
<tr><td>3 ²</td><td>9 ⁸</td><td></td><td>4</td></tr>
</table>

Student Guide - page 73

Student Guide (p. 74)

4. Maruta traded 1 skinny for 10 bits. Therefore the 5 skinnies were changed to 4. The 6 bits she started with changed to 16 bits after the trade.

5. She could not take away 6 skinnies from 4 skinnies. She traded 1 flat for 10 skinnies. Therefore the 7 flats were changed to 6 flats. The 4 skinnies she had were changed to 14 skinnies after the trade.

6. 8014 pieces of penny candy

7. 3226 more pieces of candy

8. 8191 pieces of candy

Student Guide - page 74

Student Guide (p. 75)

9. Answers will vary.

10. Art had more at the end of the week. He bought more than the combined total of those he sold and those that died.*

11. $14,381

12. $4357; Monday and Thursday's combined total = $10,024

13. $146

14. Problems will vary.

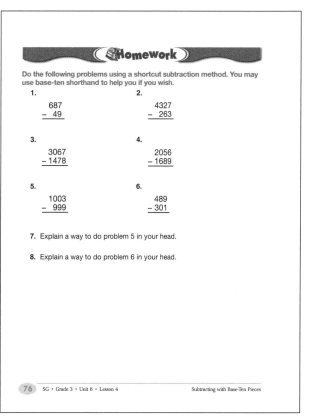

9. Make up and solve two of your own problems about penny candy sales at Art's Dime Store.

10. Art's Dime Store has four large tanks of goldfish. Here are Art's inventory records for the goldfish last week:

Number of goldfish at beginning of week	588
Number of new goldfish Art bought from his supplier	603
Number of goldfish sold to customers	462
Number of goldfish that died	81

At the end of the week, did Art have more or fewer goldfish than he had at the beginning of the week? Explain.

Art has to keep careful records of all his sales. Here are the daily total sales for the store during the first week in April.

Day of the Week Sale	Sales (in dollars)
Monday	5271
Tuesday	3008
Wednesday	3065
Thursday	4753
Friday	4329
Saturday	8297
Sunday	6084

11. The busiest days for the store are usually on the weekend. What were the sales for Saturday and Sunday together?

12. How much more were the combined sales of Saturday and Sunday than the combined sales of the next two busiest days?

13. During the same week last year, the store's sales on Tuesday were $2862. How much more did Art's Dime Store sell this year on Tuesday?

14. Make up and solve your own problems about sales at Art's Dime Store.

Subtracting with Base-Ten Pieces   SG • Grade 3 • Unit 6 • Lesson 4   75

Student Guide - page 75

Student Guide (p. 76)

Solution strategies will vary.

1. 638
2. 4064
3. 1589
4. 367
5. 4
6. 188
7. count up from 999 to 1003
8. count up from 300 to 489 (300 to 400 is 100; 400 to 489 is 89 more; 189 − 1 is 188.)

Homework

Do the following problems using a shortcut subtraction method. You may use base-ten shorthand to help you if you wish.

1.
```
  687
-  49
```

2.
```
  4327
-  263
```

3.
```
  3067
- 1478
```

4.
```
  2056
- 1689
```

5.
```
  1003
-  999
```

6.
```
  489
- 301
```

7. Explain a way to do problem 5 in your head.

8. Explain a way to do problem 6 in your head.

76   SG • Grade 3 • Unit 6 • Lesson 4   Subtracting with Base-Ten Pieces

Student Guide - page 76

*Answers and/or discussion are included in the Lesson Guide.

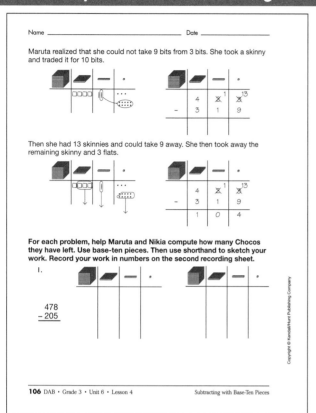

Discovery Assignment Book - page 106

Discovery Assignment Book (p. 106)

Subtracting on the Base-Ten Board

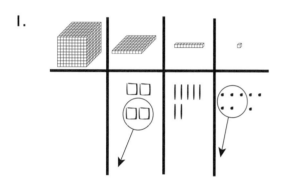

Discovery Assignment Book (p. 107)

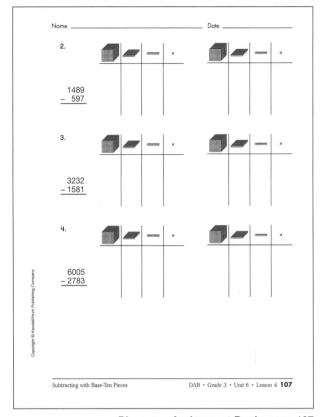

Discovery Assignment Book - page 107

2.

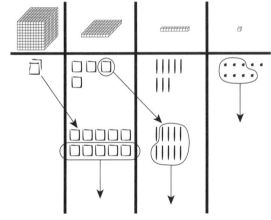

0 1	13 4	18 8	9
−	5	9	7
8	9	2	

3.

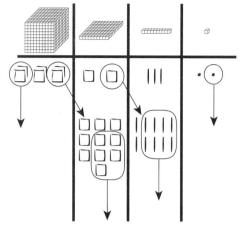

		2	11 1	13	
		3	2	3	2
−		1	5	8	1
		1	6	5	1

4.

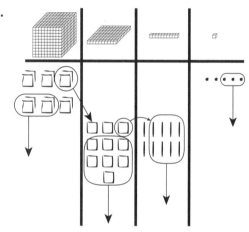

		5	10 9	10	
		6	0	0	5
−		2	7	8	3
		3	2	2	2

Discovery Assignment Book (p. 108)

Homework

Solution strategies will vary.

I. 425   2. 37

3. 55   4. 756

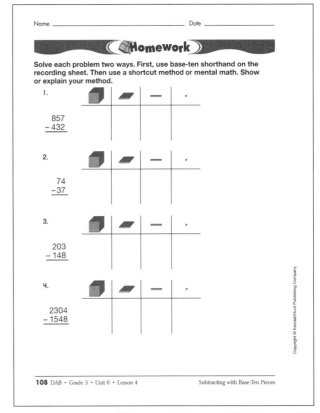

Discovery Assignment Book - page 108

Lesson 5

Close Enough!

Estimated Class Sessions

3

Lesson Overview

Students further their number sense and learn about finding and using "nice" numbers in computational estimation.

Key Content

- Developing number sense.
- Using convenient numbers to estimate.
- Developing mental math skills.

Key Vocabulary

- estimate
- estimation
- front-end estimation
- nice numbers
- rounding

Math Facts

DPP Task V provides practice with math facts.

Homework

Assign the Homework section in the *Student Guide.*

Assessment

Use the *Observational Assessment Record* to note students' abilities to estimate sums and differences using convenient numbers.

Materials List

Supplies and Copies

Student	Teacher
Supplies for Each Student Pair or Group of Three • base-ten pieces: 14 flats, 30 skinnies (rods), and 50 bits (units)	**Supplies** • base-ten pieces
Copies • 2 copies of *Hundreds Template* per student pair or more as needed (*Unit Resource Guide* Page 88)	**Copies/Transparencies** • 2 transparencies of *Hundreds Template* or more as needed (*Unit Resource Guide* Page 88)

All blackline masters including assessment, transparency, and DPP masters are also on the Teacher Resource CD.

Student Books
Close Enough! (*Student Guide* Pages 77–80)

Daily Practice and Problems and Home Practice
DPP items U–Z (*Unit Resource Guide* Pages 23–24)

Note: Classrooms whose pacing differs significantly from the suggested pacing of the units should use the Math Facts Calendar in Section 4 of the *Facts Resource Guide* to ensure students receive the complete math facts program.

Assessment Tools
Observational Assessment Record (*Unit Resource Guide* Pages 13–14)

Daily Practice and Problems

Suggestions for using the DPPs are on page 86.

U. Bit: Shortcut Addition (URG p. 23)

Do the following problems using a shortcut method. You may use base-ten shorthand if you wish.

1. $\begin{array}{r} 76 \\ +27 \\ \hline \end{array}$
2. $\begin{array}{r} 617 \\ +\ 75 \\ \hline \end{array}$

3. $\begin{array}{r} 159 \\ +345 \\ \hline \end{array}$
4. $\begin{array}{r} 809 \\ +151 \\ \hline \end{array}$

5. Explain another strategy for answering Question 4.

X. Challenge: Addition Squares (URG p. 24)

Draw boxes on your paper like these. Fill in the boxes using the digits 5, 6, 7, and 8. Use each digit only once.

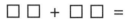

1. What is the largest sum you can get?
2. What is the smallest sum you can get?
3. How many different sums can you find?

V. Task: Story Solving (URG p. 23)

Write a story and draw a picture about 8×9. Write a number sentence on your picture.

Y. Bit: Forest Fires (URG p. 24)

On an average day, 166 forest fires start. Lightning starts 85 of these fires. How many are started by something other than lightning?

Are more than half the fires started by lightning?

W. Bit: More Change (URG p. 23)

1. How much change from $1.00 do you get if you pay 79¢ for a folder?
2. How much change from $5.00 do you get if you pay $1.79 for a hamburger?

Z. Challenge: Books (URG p. 24)

Estimate how many books are in your classroom right now. Explain how you came up with your estimate.

Teaching the Activity

This lesson has two parts. In Part 1 students use a visual approach to develop a conceptual understanding of rounding numbers to the nearest ten and hundred. In Part 2 students are introduced to strategies for estimating sums.

Part 1 Rounding Using Base-Ten Pieces

Ask student pairs to tape two copies of the *Hundreds Template* Transparency Master together as shown in Figure 22.

Use the transparencies of the *Hundreds Template* Transparency Master. Lay four flats on the grids and ask students to do the same. Ask them to count *100, 200, 300, 400.* Remind the class that they are skip counting by hundreds. Now remove the four flats and place one flat on the template. Ask:

- *How many bits are in one flat?* (100)

Now place 1 skinny on the first row of the second hundreds grid.

- *How many bits now?* (110)

Ask students to place skinnies down and count by tens along with you, until they reach 400 or run out of skinnies. Ask students to record the numbers at the end of each row as shown in Figure 22.

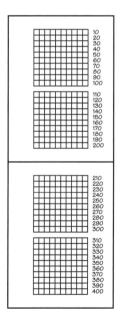

Figure 22: *Labeling 10 to 400 on the template*

Now place 1 flat, 2 skinnies, and 3 bits on the template, filling it in from the top and from left to right. Ask:

- *How many bits are on the board?* (123)
- *Is 123 closer to 100 or 200?* (100)
- *123 is between which tens?* (120 and 130)
- *Which ten is it closer to?* (120)

Ask students to count out 167 on the template. Ask:

- *167 is between which hundreds?* (100 and 200)
- *Which hundred is 167 closer to?* (200)
- *167 is between which tens?* (160 and 170)
- *Which ten is it closer to?* (170)

Continue these types of problems choosing a variety of numbers such as 329, 303, 199, 216, 98, or 300. Make sure students focus on both hundreds and tens and on which hundred or ten is closer.

Discuss the terms rounding up (the closest hundred or ten that is bigger than the given number) and rounding down (the closest hundred or ten that is smaller than the given number). For now, numbers that end in 5 or 50 can be rounded to either extreme. Later, we will discuss the convention of rounding these numbers up.

To work with numbers above 400, either ask children to imagine they have more templates or give them extra copies of the *Hundreds Template*. Use numbers above 400 such as 456, 478, 529, or 872. For each number, ask them to say the hundreds and tens that the number is between and which hundred and ten it is closest to.

Place an assortment of base-ten pieces, such as 2 flats, 8 skinnies, and 15 bits, on the overhead. Turn it on and off to flash the pieces. Ask students to estimate the number. Ask questions such as:

- *Is the number more than 200?* (Yes, I saw 2 flats and other pieces.)
- *About how many skinnies did you see? 2? 4? 5?* (Probably more than 5, about 7 or so.)
- *Do you think there are more than 10 bits? 20?* (About 10 or 11 maybe.)
- *What number do you think I flashed?* (270 or 280)

Repeat with other assortments of pieces.

Part 2 **Strategies for Computational Estimation**

Ask students to read the vignette and discuss *Question 1* on the *Close Enough!* Activity Pages in the *Student Guide.* Point out that calculators are not always handy and an estimate is a good way to get an idea of an amount. When estimating in our heads, it is easier to work with nice numbers (or **convenient numbers**) such as 10, 50, or 100.

Content Note

Depending on the context, a variety of rounding techniques can be used. In some situations, students will round up, round down, or use "convenient numbers." Convenient numbers make a problem easier to do. For example, when fifth-grade students are given the problem, 465 ÷ 60, they may decide to round 465 to 480 instead of to the nearest ten. In this case 480 ÷ 60 is much easier than 470 ÷ 60.

Some students may find the actual sum instead of an estimate. This is fine, but point out that future problems may be too difficult to solve mentally or students may not always have enough time to find the exact answers. Ask for other methods.

For *Question 2,* some students may say that 312 is close to 300 (point out that 300 is the closest 100), 542 is close to 500, and 365 is close to 400. One estimate is $300 + 500 + 400 = 1200$. (Note that since 542 is rounded down to 500 and 365 is rounded up to 400, the estimate should be pretty close.)

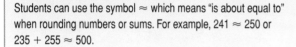

Content Note

Students can use the symbol ≈ which means "is about equal to" when rounding numbers or sums. For example, 241 ≈ 250 or $235 + 255 ≈ 500$.

There are other ways to estimate this sum as well. Another way is to use closest tens or other convenient numbers such as 5s, 25s, or 50s. This can be more difficult for some people to do in their heads. Another good estimate would be: $300 + 550 + 350 = 1200$. Students might prefer **front-end estimation,** in which only the left-most digits are used to make an estimate. For example, $312 + 542 + 365 ≈ 300 + 500 + 300$. The estimate is 1100, which is the lowest acceptable estimate. Ask:

- *Why do we say this is the lowest acceptable estimate?* (Because we rounded each number down. None of the tens or ones are included in the estimate.)

Explain to the class that you have used the word "estimate" in many ways. Note that the word is a verb (**Estimate** this sum) and a noun (Here is the **estimate**). We can estimate a number, such as 312, to be about 300 and we can also estimate a sum.

To practice estimation, give students several more problems. For example:

> *Laura is at the store and wants to buy milk for $2.05 a gallon, yogurt for $0.75, and a box of breakfast cereal for $3.85. About how much money will Laura spend?*

You may suggest that children estimate to the nearest dollar but emphasize that people often round up when at the grocery store so they do not find themselves without enough money at the checkout counter. Discuss the estimates children present. For example, $2.00 + $1.00 + $4.00 = $7.00 or $2.00 + $0.75 + $4.00 = $6.75, and so on. The students can complete *Question 3* for practice in rounding to the nearest 10 and 100.

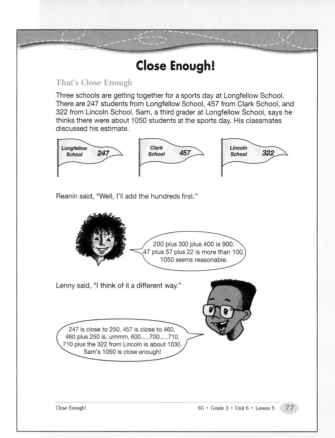

Student Guide - page 77

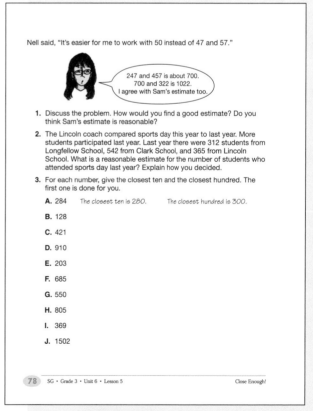

Student Guide - page 78 (Answers on p. 89)

Homework

The following problems arose when the teachers and students were producing the play "Michael and the Land of Many Colors." Help them by solving the problems.

Estimate an answer. Then solve the problem. Decide if your answer is reasonable. Explain how you solved the problem.

1. It was opening night of the play. The students in two classes decorated the auditorium with balloons. Ms. Angelo's class used 156 balloons. Mr. Sullivan's class used 138 balloons.

   A. Estimate the total number of balloons blown up by the two classes. Do you think the total is closer to 200, 300, or 400? Why?

   B. Exactly how many balloons did they blow up?

2. Silvia and Mario each hold a teddy bear in the play. The front of each teddy bear needs to be covered with fancy material. Silvia measured her teddy bear. She found that it needed 1235 square centimeters of fancy material. Mario measured his teddy bear. He found that it needed 73 square centimeters more than Silvia's bear.

   A. Estimate the amount of material needed for Mario's bear. Is it closest to 1200, 1250, or 1300 square centimeters?

   B. Exactly how much material did Mario's bear need?

3. To make the scenery, they had to measure the distance across the stage. Naomi and Dave measured the stage. Naomi began measuring from the right side and Dave from the left. When they met, Naomi had measured 327 cm and Dave had measured 273 cm. What is the distance across the stage?

Close Enough!   SG · Grade 3 · Unit 6 · Lesson 5   79

Student Guide - page 79 *(Answers on p. 89)*

---

4. Students sold tickets to two performances of the play. Students sold 385 advance tickets for the first performance. They sold 656 advance tickets for both performances combined.

   A. Do you think that more tickets were sold for the first performance or the second performance? Why?

   B. How many tickets were sold for the second performance?

   C. The auditorium has 400 seats. How many tickets will they have left to sell at the door at each of the two performances?

5. The students held a bake sale to raise extra money to pay for the costumes. Students brought in cookies for the bake sale. Ms. Angelo's class brought in 194 cookies, and Mr. Sullivan's class brought in 235.

   A. If Ms. Angelo's class brought in 100 more cookies, would they have more cookies than Mr. Sullivan's class?

   B. How many extra cookies would Ms. Angelo's class need to equal the same number as Mr. Sullivan's class?

6. The bake sale earned $253. Students used $185 to buy material for the costumes.

   A. After buying the material, did the students have more or less than $100 left from the bake sale money?

   B. Exactly how much money did they have left?

7. Solve the following problems using any method you choose. Estimate to be sure your answer is reasonable.

   A.
   $$377$$
   $$+\ 451$$

   B.
   $$621$$
   $$-\ 557$$

   C.
   $$805$$
   $$-\ 626$$

8. Explain your estimation strategy for Question 7B.

80   SG · Grade 3 · Unit 6 · Lesson 5   Close Enough!

Student Guide - page 80 *(Answers on p. 90)*

Math Facts

For DPP Task V students write a story and draw a picture to illustrate a multiplication fact.

Homework and Practice

- Assign the Homework section of the *Close Enough!* Activity Pages. On completion, choose one or two questions to discuss estimation strategies.

- DPP Bit U provides practice with addition using paper and pencil. Bit W is computation with money. Items X, Y, and Z build number sense and skills in computation and estimation.

Assessment

Use the class discussion of estimation strategies students used to complete the Homework section to assess their progress in using convenient numbers to estimate. Record your observations on the *Observational Assessment Record.*

At a Glance

Math Facts and Daily Practice and Problems

DPP Task V provides practice with math facts. Items U, W, X, and Y provide computation practice. Challenge Z is an estimation problem.

Part 1. Rounding Using Base-Ten Pieces

1. Student pairs tape two copies of the *Hundreds Template* Transparency Master together.
2. Students lay flats on the grids and count 100, 200, 300, 400.
3. Students lay skinnies on the grids to represent numbers between 100 and 400.
4. Students discuss between which tens and hundreds a number lies. They also find the closest ten and the closest hundred.
5. Repeat with numbers greater than 400.
6. Students estimate the number of base-ten pieces flashed on the overhead.

Part 2. Strategies for Computational Estimation

1. Students complete *Questions 1–3* in the *Student Guide.*
2. Discuss different ways of estimating and finding convenient numbers.
3. Students solve estimation word problems.

Homework

Assign the Homework section in the *Student Guide.*

Assessment

Use the *Observational Assessment Record* to note students' abilities to estimate sums and differences using convenient numbers.

Answer Key is on pages 89–90.

Notes:

Hundreds Template

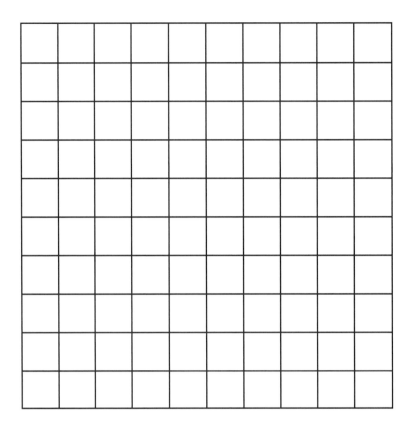

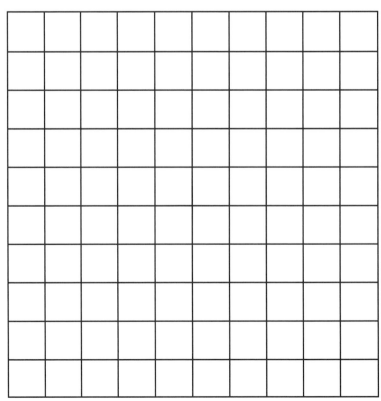

Student Guide (p. 78)

1. Solution strategies will vary. Yes.*

2. Estimates will vary; 1100, 1200, and 1250 are three appropriate estimates. See Lesson Guide 5 for how these estimates were found.*

3. A. 280; 300

   B. 130; 100

   C. 420; 400

   D. 910; 900

   E. 200; 200

   F. 680 or 690; 700

   G. 550; 500 or 600

   H. 800 or 810; 800

   I. 370; 400

   J. 1500; 1500

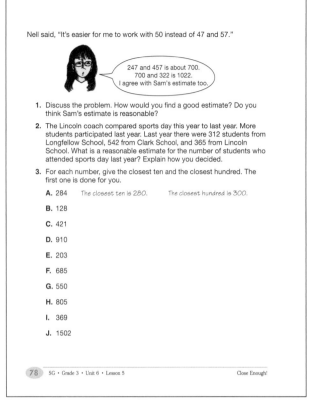

Student Guide - page 78

Student Guide (p. 79)

Homework

1. A. about 300 balloons; 156 is close to 160; 138 is close to 140

   B. 294 balloons

2. A. 1300 square centimeters; explanations will vary. Possible response:

   1235 is close to 1230; 73 is close to 70; 1230 + 70 = 1300

   B. 1308 square centimeters

3. 600 cm

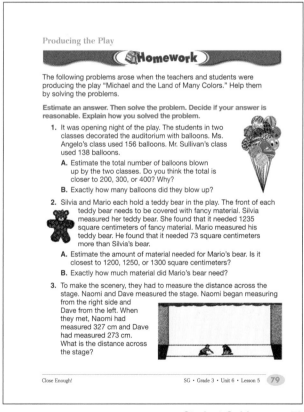

Student Guide - page 79

*Answers and/or discussion are included in the Lesson Guide.

4. Students sold tickets to two performances of the play. Students sold 385 advance tickets for the first performance. They sold 656 advance tickets for both performances combined.

A. Do you think that more tickets were sold for the first performance or the second performance? Why?

B. How many tickets were sold for the second performance?

C. The auditorium has 400 seats. How many tickets will they have left to sell at the door at each of the two performances?

5. The students held a bake sale to raise extra money to pay for the costumes. Students brought in cookies for the bake sale. Ms. Angelo's class brought in 194 cookies, and Mr. Sullivan's class brought in 235.

A. If Ms. Angelo's class brought in 100 more cookies, would they have more cookies than Mr. Sullivan's class?

B. How many extra cookies would Ms. Angelo's class need to equal the same number as Mr. Sullivan's class?

6. The bake sale earned $253. Students used $185 to buy material for the costumes.

A. After buying the material, did the students have more or less than $100 left from the bake sale money?

B. Exactly how much money did they have left?

7. Solve the following problems using any method you choose. Estimate to be sure your answer is reasonable.

A.
$$377 + 451$$

B.
$$621 - 557$$

C.
$$805 - 626$$

8. Explain your estimation strategy for Question 7B.

Student Guide - page 80

Student Guide (p. 80)

4. **A.** First performance; 385 is close to 400; 400 is more than halfway to 656

B. 271 tickets

C. First performance will have 15 seats available. Second performance will have 129 seats available.

5. **A.** Yes; they would have almost 300 cookies.

B. 41 cookies

6. **A.** Less; 185 is close to 200; 253 is close to 250. They'd have about $50 left.

B. $68

7. **A.** 828

B. 64

C. 179

8. Strategies will vary. Possible response:
$$625 - 550 = 75$$

Lesson 6

Leonardo the Blockhead

Lesson Overview

Estimated Class Sessions

1

Leonardo the Blockhead is about the great Italian mathematician Fibonacci and his role in introducing Hindu-Arabic numeration and associated algorithms to Europe. This story is based on fact. The hero, Leonardo, is known today as Fibonacci. He was born in Pisa about 1170 and died about 1250 and is considered the greatest mathematician of the Middle Ages. Fibonacci is most famous for a certain number sequence (1, 1, 2, 3, 5, 8, 13, . . .) he investigated and today bears his name.

The basic outline of the story is historically accurate: Leonardo's father really was a merchant, and Leonardo did live in Bugia and did travel in North Africa and the Middle East. On these travels he came into contact with Arab mathematicians who were more advanced at that time than European mathematicians.

In particular, Leonardo learned about Hindu-Arabic numeration and wrote about the new system in his *Liber Abaci,* Book of the Abacus, published in 1202. Finally, Leonardo really did sign his name Bigollo, although the exact reason is unclear. The details in the story of Leonardo's discussions with his parents and the Arabs, however, are fictionalized.

Key Content

- Understanding the historical and multicultural roots of the Hindu-Arabic number system.
- Reviewing paper-and-pencil algorithms for addition and subtraction.
- Connecting mathematics and social studies.

Key Vocabulary

- abacus

Assessment

Use DPP Bit AA as an assessment of students' progress with subtraction.

Materials List

Supplies and Copies

Student	Teacher
Supplies for Each Student	**Supplies** • map of Europe, North Africa, and the Middle East, optional
Copies	**Copies/Transparencies**

All blackline masters including assessment, transparency, and DPP masters are also on the Teacher Resource CD.

Student Books
Leonardo the Blockhead (*Adventure Book* Pages 43–58)

Daily Practice and Problems and Home Practice
DPP items AA–BB (*Unit Resource Guide* Page 25)

Note: Classrooms whose pacing differs significantly from the suggested pacing of the units should use the Math Facts Calendar in Section 4 of the *Facts Resource Guide* to ensure students receive the complete math facts program.

Daily Practice and Problems

Suggestions for using the DPPs are on page 100.

AA. Bit: Shortcut Subtraction

(URG p. 25)

Do the following problems using a shortcut method.
You can use base-ten shorthand if you want.

1. 147
    − 36

2. 563
    − 125

3. 2750
    − 129

4. 5007
    − 4997

5. Explain a way to do Question 4 in your head.

BB. Task: Measuring Ourselves

(URG p. 25)

Find a partner. Measure to find out how
tall you and your partner are in centimeters.

1. Who is taller? How much taller?

2. If you stood on your partner's shoulders,
   how tall would you both be?

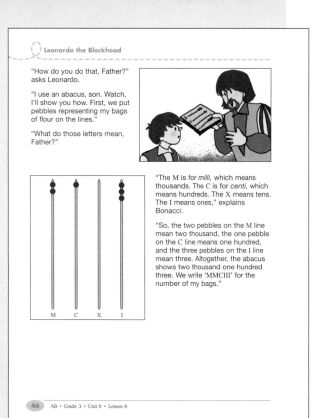

Adventure Book - page 46

The story refers to various locations in Europe, North Africa, and the Middle East. Point out these places on a map or globe before beginning the story.

Discussion Prompts

Page 46

Bonacci's abacus can also be called a counting board. The pebbles are not fixed on wires as on modern abacuses, but are removable and placed in grooves incised on the board's surface. We get our word *counter* from the custom of embedding such counting boards into tabletops in stores. The word *calculate* comes from the Latin *calculi,* pebbles, from the use of pebbles on such counting boards.

- *What English words come from the Latin word parts* milli- *and* centi-?

- *How would you show 4507 on an abacus? 2901?*

- *How does showing numbers on an abacus compare to showing numbers using base-ten pieces?*

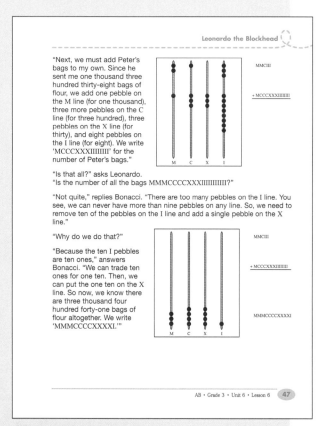

Adventure Book - page 47

Page 47

The version of Roman numerals used in the story is simplified. No use is made of two features normally seen in Roman numerals: positional subtraction (e.g., IX = X − I) and letters that are not powers of ten (V, L, etc.). This simplified version is, however, quite functional and has some historical basis.

- *Can you write three hundred one in Roman numerals? How about one hundred three?*

- *How do Roman numerals compare to our way of writing numbers?*

Regrouping and multiple partitioning of numbers are major themes in this story, so there are many opportunities for discussion.

- *How is what Bonacci does (when he trades ten ones-pebble for one tens-pebble) like the Fewest Pieces Rule?*

- *Can you use base-ten pieces or numbers to solve Bonacci's problem (2103 + 1338)?*

Page 49

- *How can the same mark, 3, sometimes mean three hundred and other times three?*
- *Do you think Hindu-Arabic numbers are easier than Roman numerals?*
- *Why does Leonardo's father say, "Don't be a blockhead"?*
- *Where is Pisa? In what modern country is Pisa? What famous building is in Pisa?* (Italy, The Leaning Tower of Pisa)

Adventure Book - page 49

Page 50

- *What is the number on the top part of the abacus? What is the number on the bottom?*

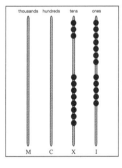

Adventure Book - page 50

Leonardo the Blockhead

"Next, we add the 5 and the 7. That makes twelve. But remember, twelve is really one ten and two ones," explains Ali. "So, we write the '2' below the line in the ones place and put the '1' in the tens place above the line."

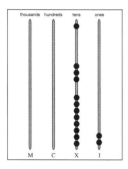

thousands hundreds tens ones

M   C   X   I

"That's like trading pebbles on the abacus," says Leonardo. "We trade ten ones pebbles for one tens pebble."

"Then what do you do?" asks Ali.

AB • Grade 3 • Unit 6 • Lesson 6   51

Adventure Book - page 51

Page 51

- *Explain what Leonardo means when he says, "That's like trading pebbles on the abacus. We trade ten ones-pebbles for one tens-pebble."*

Leonardo the Blockhead

"On the abacus, we would have to trade again," says Leonardo, "since there are too many on the tens line. We trade ten tens pebbles for one hundreds pebble. So, the answer is one hundred twenty-two."

"What we do is similar," says Ali. "The next thing we do is to add the tens. We have 1 + 3 + 8 tens."

"That's twelve tens," says Leonardo.

"But twelve tens are 10 tens and 2 tens," says Ali. "How much are 10 tens?"

"Ten tens make one hundred," says Leonardo. "Is the hundreds place just to the left of the tens place?"

thousands hundreds tens ones

M   C   X   I

"Yes, exactly. You learn quickly," says Ali. "The 12 tens are 1 hundred and 2 tens, so we put a 1 in the hundreds place and a 2 in the tens place. The answer is 122."

"That's wonderful!" exclaims Leonardo. "Show me another!"

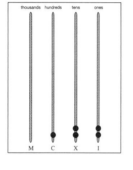

52   AB • Grade 3 • Unit 6 • Lesson 6

Adventure Book - page 52

Page 52

- *What are twelve tens?*
- *Try some other problems like 37 + 85. Show how to solve them on an abacus and also using Hindu-Arabic numerals.*

Page 53

- *Do you agree that "Subtraction is a little harder, but you will learn it if you try"?*
- *Can you solve the problem 84 − 25 using base-ten pieces?*

Adventure Book - page 53

Page 54

Some children have trouble "lining up the places." Ask students what would be wrong about writing problems this way:

$$\begin{array}{r} 87 \\ +\ 9 \\ \hline \end{array} \qquad \begin{array}{r} 56 \\ +124 \\ \hline \end{array}$$

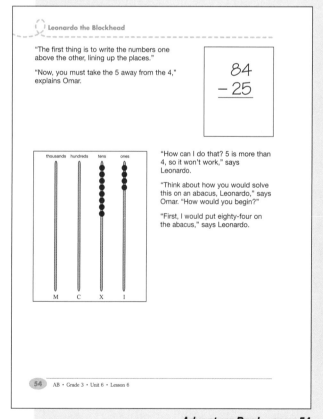

Adventure Book - page 54

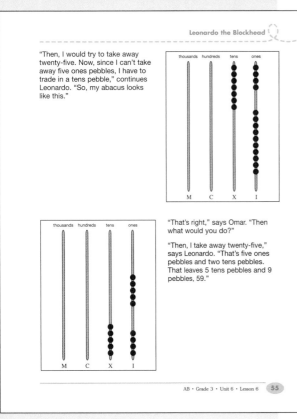

Adventure Book - page 55

Page 55

- *How many tens and how many ones does the abacus show?* (7 tens and 14 ones)
- *Does the abacus still show a number that is equal to 84?* (yes)
- *Can you write a number sentence for what the abacus shows?* (70 + 14 = 84)

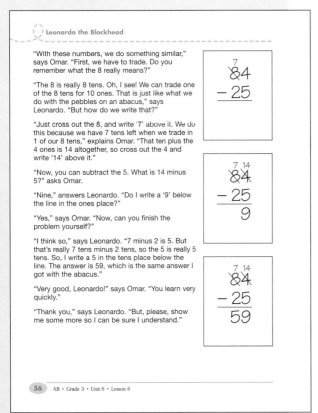

Adventure Book - page 56

Page 56

- *What does the 7 above the crossed-out 8 stand for?* (7 tens or 70)
- *What about that little 14 above the 4?* (14 ones)
- *Can you write a number sentence to show what the top number is?* (70 + 14 = 84)
- *Compare the steps on the abacus and the steps using the Hindu-Arabic numerals. How are they alike? Different?*

Pause here and let some children take turns pretending to be Leonardo to see whether they can solve a few problems on a slate, on chart paper, or at the board or overhead.

Page 57

- *Find Syria and Greece on the map on page 53.*
- *Can you use the Arabic numerals to add 37 and 68?*

Leonardo spends more time in Syria and travels to Greece as well. Everywhere, he learns more mathematics from the Arabs.

Finally, he goes home. His family is very happy to have him back.

Leonardo is excited about all he has learned and tries to explain it to his father and mother.

"Father," says Leonardo, "we should use the Arabic numerals for our business. They are easier than an abacus. Let me show you how. Suppose we want to add thirty-seven and sixty-eight…"

Leonardo teaches his parents and others how to use the new way of writing numbers.

AB • Grade 3 • Unit 6 • Lesson 6   57

Adventure Book - page 57

Page 58

- *Do you think Leonardo was a blockhead?*

Leonardo the Blockhead

Soon, Leonardo writes a book of mathematics which he calls *The Book of the Abacus*. He explains the new way of writing numbers and how to use them to add and subtract. He also invents much mathematics of his own. People all over Europe learn from his book.

Leonardo writes many more books of mathematics.

Sometimes, Leonardo signs his name Leonardo Bigollo.

This can mean two things, Leonardo the Traveler or Leonardo the Blockhead. Today, people think Leonardo meant to make a joke. He surely did like to travel, but they think he called himself a blockhead to poke fun at the people who thought he was foolish. He was really one of the greatest mathematicians of his time.

Today, we don't call him Leonardo the Blockhead. We know him as Fibonacci, which means "son of Bonacci."

58   AB • Grade 3 • Unit 6 • Lesson 6

Adventure Book - page 58

Homework and Practice

Task BB is a word problem that applies measurement skills.

Assessment

Use DPP Bit AA as an assessment of students' progress with subtraction.

Resources

- Berggren, J.L. *Episodes in the Mathematics of Medieval Islam.* Springer-Verlag, New York, 1986.

- Eves, Howard W. *In Mathematical Circles: A Selection of Mathematical Stories and Anecdotes* (Quadrants I, II, III and IV). Prindle, Weber & Schmidt, Inc., Boston, 1969.

- Ifrah, Georges. *The Universal History of Numbers: From Prehistory to the Invention of the Computer.* John Wiley & Sons, Hoboken, NJ, 1999.

- Lumpkin, Beatrice. "African and African-American Contributions to Mathematics." In *African American Baseline Essays.* Portland Public Schools, Portland, OR, 1987.

- Menninger, Karl. *Number Words and Number Symbols: A Cultural History of Numbers.* Dover Publications, New York, 1992.

- Nelson, David, George Gheverghese Joseph, and Julian Williams. *Multicultural Mathematics: Teaching Mathematics from a Global Perspective.* Oxford University Press, New York, 1993.

- Smith, David Eugene. *History of Mathematics.* Volume I. Dover Publications, New York, 1951.

Lesson 7

Palindromes

Lesson Overview

Students practice addition with two-, three-, and four-digit numbers. At the same time they discover number patterns as they explore palindromes.

Key Content

- Practicing addition with two-, three-, and four-digit numbers.
- Identifying number patterns.

Key Vocabulary

- palindrome

Math Facts

DPP Challenge DD provides practice with multiplication facts and computation.

Homework

Assign Parts 3 and 4 of the Home Practice.

Assessment

Use the *Observational Assessment Record* to note students' abilities to add using paper and pencil.

Materials List

Supplies and Copies

Student	Teacher
Supplies for Each Student • colored markers or crayons • calculator **Supplies for Each Student Pair or Group of Three** • 1 set of base-ten pieces	**Supplies**
Copies • 1 copy of *100 Chart* per student (*Unit Resource Guide* Page 107)	**Copies/Transparencies** • 1 transparency of *100 Chart* (*Unit Resource Guide* Page 107)

All blackline masters including assessment, transparency, and DPP masters are also on the Teacher Resource CD.

Daily Practice and Problems and Home Practice

DPP items CC–DD (*Unit Resource Guide* Pages 25–26)
Home Practice Parts 3–4 (*Discovery Assignment Book* Page 101)

Note: Classrooms whose pacing differs significantly from the suggested pacing of the units should use the Math Facts Calendar in Section 4 of the *Facts Resource Guide* to ensure students receive the complete math facts program.

Assessment Tools

Observational Assessment Record (*Unit Resource Guide* Pages 13–14)

Daily Practice and Problems

Suggestions for using the DPPs are on page 105.

CC. Bit: More Raincoats (URG p. 25)

Joe the Goldfish has two cousins, Zelda the Zebra Fish and Angie the Angel Fish. Zelda has a raincoat made with 1793 sq cm of material. Angie's raincoat is 288 sq cm bigger than Zelda's.

Did it take more than 2000 sq cm of material to make Angie's raincoat?

What is the exact area of Angie's raincoat?

DD. Challenge: Jonah's Class Project (URG p. 26)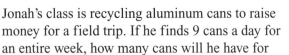

Jonah's class is recycling aluminum cans to raise money for a field trip. If he finds 9 cans a day for an entire week, how many cans will he have for his class?

The class needs $3 more to pay for the bus. If Jonah receives 5 cents for each can he collected during the week, will they have enough?

This activity provides a fun context for practice with addition. As students explore palindromes and record their results on a *100 Chart*, interesting and valuable patterns will emerge.

A **palindrome** is a number or word or phrase that reads the same forward and backward—44, 363, 2112, and 12321 are examples of number palindromes. Otto, wow, and toot are examples of words that are palindromes. "Madam I'm Adam" and "Must sell at tallest sum" are examples of phrases that are palindromes.

The number 134 is *not* a palindrome. However, by doing some addition, a palindrome can be created from 134. If you write 134 backwards (431) and add it to 134, you get a palindrome (565). This is shown in Figure 23. Because a palindrome is made from 134 after one such step, we call this a one-step palindrome.

```
  134    Original number
+ 431    Add the number written backwards
  565    A palindrome!
```

Figure 23: *A one-step palindrome*

Some numbers take more steps to make a palindrome. 86, for example, is a three-step palindrome. (See Figure 24.)

```
   86    Original number
 + 68    Add the number written backwards
  154    Still not a palindrome
+ 451    Add the new sum written backwards
  605    Still not a palindrome
+ 506    Add the new sum written backwards
 1111    A palindrome!
```

Figure 24: *A three-step palindrome*

Once students understand what a palindrome is and how to find multistep palindromes, let them see whether they can find some palindromes (i.e., one-step palindromes, two-step palindromes, three-step palindromes, etc.). Tell them to save their work.

Pass out the *100 Chart*. Ask students to color each number on the chart a different color depending on how many steps it takes to make a palindrome from that number. For example, students can color all palindromes (e.g., 11, 66, all one-digit numbers) blue; all one-step palindromes green; all two-step palindromes yellow; and so on until all numbers, 1–100, are colored.

All the numbers 1–100 are palindromes in 6 or fewer steps except for 89 and 98. It takes 24 steps to convert 89 and 98 into palindromes! The resulting palindrome is 8,813,200,023,188. You may want to tell your students to skip those two numbers or make it a challenge problem.

As students begin filling in the *100 Chart,* they will see patterns and can use the patterns to find various shortcuts for filling in the chart. Encourage them to make predictions based on the patterns.

Since the major goal of the activity is to develop fluency with addition, encourage students to solve most of the problems without a calculator. (You can call this a "dead battery day.") They can use mental arithmetic, paper and pencil, base-ten pieces, or other strategies. However, calculators can be made available for checking results, working on some of the more difficult problems, or generally exploring palindromes.

Students can complete the activity in class or as a homework assignment. It can be done in one day or spread over several days.

Journal Prompt

Describe the patterns on your palindrome chart. Why do you think that these patterns exist?
or
What shortcuts did you use when you filled in your palindrome chart?

Math Facts

DPP Challenge DD provides practice with math facts and with computation.

Homework and Practice

- DPP Bit CC is a word problem that builds estimation and computation skills.
- Assign Parts 3 and 4 of the Home Practice as homework. They contain computation and number sense problems.

Answers for Parts 3 and 4 of the Home Practice are in the Answer Key at the end of this lesson and at the end of this unit.

Assessment

Use the *Observational Assessment Record* to note students' abilities to add using paper and pencil.

Extension

Students can find palindromes with larger numbers or find words that are palindromes.

Literature Connections

- Bergenson, Howard W. *Palindromes and Anagrams.* Dover Publications, New York, 1973.
- Terban, Marvin. *Too Hot to Hoot.* Clarion Books, New York, 1985.

Name _____ Date _____

PART 3

1. Mario covered a piece of paper with base-ten pieces. He used 4 flats and 16 skinnies. Beth said, "That's the same as 416 bits." Is Beth correct? Why or why not? Use base-ten shorthand to show your answer.

2. The middle school collected 1321 canned goods for a charity. The junior high school collected 1299 cans. The high school collected 2219 canned goods.

   A. Which school collected the most canned goods? _____

   B. Which school collected the least? _____

   C. List the numbers from largest to smallest. _____

   D. How many cans were collected in all? _____

PART 4

1. A. Ann Marie has some quarters, nickels, and dimes. She has ten coins in all. Half of them are quarters.
   What is the most money Ann Marie could have? _____
   Show how you solved this problem.

   B. What is the least amount Ann Marie could have? _____
   Show how you solved this problem.

2. At the zoo, Joe's dad bought 5 snow cones, one for each family member. One snow cone costs $1.26. How much do 5 snow cones cost? _____ Show how you found your answer.

MORE ADDING AND SUBTRACTING   DAB • Grade 3 • Unit 6 **101**

Discovery Assignment Book - page 101 *(Answers on p. 108)*

At a Glance

Math Facts and Daily Practice and Problems

DPP Bit CC is a word problem. Challenge DD provides practice with multiplication facts and computatio⟩

Teaching the Activity

1. Explain what a palindrome is and give examples such as 44, 363, and 2112.
2. Show how the one-step palindrome, 565, can be formed using 134. (134 + 431 = 565)
3. Demonstrate how other palindromes such as the three-step palindrome, 1111, can be formed usin⟩ (86 + 68 = 154; 154 + 451 = 605; 605 + 506 = 1111)
4. Students work individually or in pairs to find palindromes.
5. Students color each number on the *100 Chart* to indicate how many steps it takes to make a palindrome from that number.
6. Encourage students to look for patterns and find shortcuts for filling in the chart.

Homework

Assign Parts 3 and 4 of the Home Practice.

Assessment

Use the *Observational Assessment Record* to note students' abilities to add using paper and pencil.

Extension

Students can find palindromes with larger numbers or find words that are palindromes.

Connection

Two related books to this lesson include *Palindromes and Anagrams* by Howard Bergenson and *Too H⟩ Hoot* by Marvin Terban.

Answer Key is on page 108.

Notes:

Name _____   Date _____

100 Chart

1	2	3	4	5	6	7	8	9	10
11	12	13	14	15	16	17	18	19	20
21	22	23	24	25	26	27	28	29	30
31	32	33	34	35	36	37	38	39	40
41	42	43	44	45	46	47	48	49	50
51	52	53	54	55	56	57	58	59	60
61	62	63	64	65	66	67	68	69	70
71	72	73	74	75	76	77	78	79	80
81	82	83	84	85	86	87	88	89	90
91	92	93	94	95	96	97	98	99	100

Name _____ Date _____

PART 3

1. Mario covered a piece of paper with base-ten pieces. He used 4 flats and 16 skinnies. Beth said, "That's the same as 416 bits." Is Beth correct? Why or why not? Use base-ten shorthand to show your answer.

2. The middle school collected 1321 canned goods for a charity. The junior high school collected 1299 cans. The high school collected 2219 canned goods.

   A. Which school collected the most canned goods? _____

   B. Which school collected the least? _____

   C. List the numbers from largest to smallest. _____

   D. How many cans were collected in all? _____

PART 4

1. A. Ann Marie has some quarters, nickels, and dimes. She has ten coins in all. Half of them are quarters.
   What is the most money Ann Marie could have? _____
   Show how you solved this problem.

   B. What is the least amount Ann Marie could have? _____
   Show how you solved this problem.

2. At the zoo, Joe's dad bought 5 snow cones, one for each family member. One snow cone costs $1.26. How much do 5 snow cones cost? _____ Show how you found your answer.

MORE ADDING AND SUBTRACTING   DAB • Grade 3 • Unit 6 **101**

Discovery Assignment Book - page 101

Discovery Assignment Book (p. 101)

Home Practice*

Part 3

1. No. 16 skinnies = 160 bits, not 16 bits.
   160 bits + 400 bits = 560 bits.

2. **A.** high school
   B. junior high school
   C. 2219, 1321, 1299
   D. 4839 cans

Part 4

1. **A.** $1.70 (5 quarters + 4 dimes + 1 nickel = $1.25 + $0.40 + $0.05 = $1.70)
   Strategies will vary.

   B. $1.55 (5 quarters + 4 nickels + 1 dime = $1.25 + $0.20 + $0.10 = $1.55)
   Strategies will vary.

2. $6.30 ($1.26 + $1.26 + $1.26 + $1.26 + $1.26 = $6.30)
   Strategies will vary.

*Answers for all the Home Practice in the *Discovery Assignment Book* are at the end of the unit.

Lesson 8

Digits Game

Lesson Overview

Cards are drawn one at a time from a deck of ten digit cards. Students attempt to make the largest or smallest answer to addition and subtraction problems by strategically placing the digits on a playing board. After playing the *Digits Game* together as a class, you can play it on an ongoing basis. This game provides computation practice for many items in the Daily Practice and Problems.

Key Content

• Practicing addition and subtraction of large numbers.
• Understanding place value.
• Developing number sense.

Key Vocabulary

• digit

Homework

Students can play the game at home with their families.

Assessment

1. Use the *Observational Assessment Record* to note students' abilities to add and subtract with paper and pencil.
2. Transfer appropriate assessment documentation from the Unit 6 *Observational Assessment Record* to students' *Individual Assessment Record Sheets.*

Materials List

Supplies and Copies

Student	Teacher
Supplies for Each Student Group • 10 index cards, optional	**Supplies**
Copies • 1 copy of *Digit Cards 0–9* per student group, copied back to back (*Unit Resource Guide* Pages 115–116)	**Copies/Transparencies**

All blackline masters including assessment, transparency, and DPP masters are also on the Teacher Resource CD.

Student Books
Digits Game (*Discovery Assignment Book* Page 109)

Daily Practice and Problems and Home Practice
DPP items EE–FF (*Unit Resource Guide* Page 26)

Note: Classrooms whose pacing differs significantly from the suggested pacing of the units should use the Math Facts Calendar in Section 4 of the *Facts Resource Guide* to ensure students receive the complete math facts program.

Assessment Tools
Observational Assessment Record (*Unit Resource Guide* Pages 13–14)
Individual Assessment Record Sheet (*Teacher Implementation Guide,* Assessment section)

Daily Practice and Problems

Suggestions for using the DPPs are on page 113.

EE. Bit: Play Digits: Largest Sum Ⓝ ✖
(URG p. 26)

$$\begin{array}{r} \square\ \square \\ +\ \square\ \square \\ \hline \end{array}$$

As your teacher or classmate reads the digits, place them in the boxes. Try to find the largest sum. Remember, each digit will be read only once.

FF. Task: Play Digits: Largest and Ⓝ ✖
Smallest Difference (URG p. 26)

Draw boxes on your paper like these:

$$\begin{array}{r} \square\ \square \\ -\ \square\ \square \\ \hline \end{array}$$

As your teacher or classmate reads the digits, place them in the boxes. Try to find the smallest difference. Remember each digit will be read only once. Play again, but this time find the largest difference.

Teaching the Game

To play the game, students draw boxes on their papers to get a template for an addition or subtraction problem. Using the *Digit Cards 0–9,* the teacher or game leader draws cards one at a time. Students place numbers in the boxes as each is read. Once a digit is placed, it cannot be moved. When all the boxes are filled, students find the answer to the problem. Students with the largest answer win.

The directions for the game are on the *Digits Game* page. Encourage students to think carefully as they place digits in the boxes. To place numbers advantageously, students will have to use their knowledge of place value and notions about probability. After the game is complete and students have their answers, discuss their choices for placing numbers. For example, if the playing board looks like the one in Figure 25 and the first card drawn is an 8, where should it be placed?

Figure 25: *Template for Digits Game*

One good choice is to place the 8 in the hundreds place of the top addend. This will ensure a large number. However, since there is the possibility that a 9 will also be drawn, another choice is to wait for the 9 and to place the 8 in a box in the tens place. If the 8 is placed in the tens place, does it make a difference whether it is placed in the top addend or the bottom? A discussion of where students chose to place the 8 provides opportunities for them to communicate their knowledge of place value and addition and subtraction.

Note to students that they can play the game with either addition or subtraction and either largest or smallest answers. Have students begin playing using addition and the largest answer and vary it as they get more practice.

Name _____ Date _____

Digits Game

Players

This is a game for any number of players.

Materials

- one set of ten cards with the digits 0 through 9 written on them
- paper
- pencils

Rules

The object of the game is to get the largest answer to an addition or subtraction problem.

1. One person is the leader, and the others are players. The leader draws one playing board so that all of the players can see it. The playing board is a set of boxes arranged like an addition or subtraction problem. Here are some examples of playing boards:

The leader draws only one playing board for each game.

2. Each player draws the playing board on his or her paper.
3. The leader tells the players to play for the largest answer. Then, he or she shuffles the cards, places them face down, picks the top card, and reads the digit to all the players.
4. Each player writes that digit in one of the boxes on his or her playing board. Each player must decide where to place the digit in order to get the largest answer. Once a player has written down a digit, it may not be moved. No digit will be repeated.
5. Placing the first card in a discard pile, the leader reads the next card from the top of the deck. Players place this digit in another unfilled box. Play continues until all the boxes are filled.
6. When all the boxes are filled, players add or subtract to find their answers, as indicated on the original playing board drawn by the leader. The player with the largest correct answer wins the game.

Another way to play the game is to have the smallest correct answer win the game.

Digits Game   DAB · Grade 3 · Unit 6 · Lesson 8 **109**

Discovery Assignment Book - page 109

Homework and Practice

- Encourage students to play the *Digits Game* with their families.
- Both DPP items EE and FF are examples of the *Digits Game*. Bit EE provides addition practice, and Task FF provides subtraction practice.

Assessment

- Use the *Observational Assessment Record* to note students' abilities to add and subtract using paper and pencil.
- Transfer appropriate documentation from the Unit 6 *Observational Assessment Record* to students' *Individual Assessment Record Sheets*.

At a Glance

Math Facts and Daily Practice and Problems

DPP items EE and FF both provide practice with paper-and-pencil addition and subtraction.

Teaching the Game

1. Read together the game directions on the *Digits Game* Game Page in the *Discovery Assignment Book.*
2. Students draw boxes on their papers to get a template for an addition or subtraction problem.
3. The game leader announces whether they are playing for the largest sum, largest difference, smallest sum, or smallest difference.
4. Using the *Digit Cards 0–9,* the game leader draws cards one at a time from the deck.
5. Students place the numbers in the boxes as each number is read.
6. When all the boxes are filled, students find the answer to the problem.
7. Students with the largest answers (or smallest) win.
8. Discuss students' choices for placing the numbers.

Homework

Students can play the game at home with their families.

Assessment

1. Use the *Observational Assessment Record* to note students' abilities to add and subtract with paper and pencil.
2. Transfer appropriate assessment documentation from the Unit 6 *Observational Assessment Record* to students' *Individual Assessment Record Sheets.*

Notes:

Digit Cards 0–9

4	9
3	8
2	7
1	6
0	5

Reverse Side of Digit Cards 0–9

Discovery Assignment Book (p. 100)

Part 1

I. **A.** 6   **B.** 7

    C. 5   **D.** 4

    E. 5   **F.** 9

    G. 6   **H.** 9

2. Strategies will vary. One possible strategy is to use doubles; 14 is the double of 7. Since 8 is one more than 7, the answer will be one less, 6.

Part 2

I. **A.** 210 ($56 + 54 = 110 + 100 = 210$)

     Strategies will vary.

   B. 203 ($32 - 29 = 3, 3 + 200 = 203$)

     Strategies will vary.

2. **A.** 108 carnations ($48 + 60 = 108$)

     Strategies will vary.

   B. 156 flowers ($108 + 48 = 156$)

     Strategies will vary.

Discovery Assignment Book - page 100

Discovery Assignment Book (p. 101)

Part 3

I. No; 16 skinnies = 160 bits, not 16 bits.

   160 bits + 400 bits = 560 bits

2. **A.** high school

   B. junior high school

   C. 2219, 1321, 1299

   D. 4839 cans

Part 4

I. **A.** $1.70 (5 quarters + 4 dimes + 1 nickel = $1.25 + $0.40 + $0.05 = $1.70)

     Strategies will vary.

   B. $1.55 (5 quarters + 4 nickels + 1 dime = $1.25 + $0.20 + $0.10 = $1.55)

     Strategies will vary.

2. $6.30 ($1.26 + $1.26 + $1.26 + $1.26 + $1.26 = $6.30)

     Strategies will vary.

Discovery Assignment Book - page 101

Name _____ Date _____

Unit 6 Home Practice

PART 1

I. **A.** 15 − 9 = _____   **B.** 17 − 10 = _____

   C. 9 − 4 = _____   **D.** 11 − 7 = _____

   E. 7 − 2 = _____   **F.** 12 − 3 = _____

   G. 14 − 8 = _____   **H.** 18 − 9 = _____

2. Leah has a hard time finding the answer to 1G. How did you find the answer to this subtraction fact? Share your method.

PART 2

I. Solve the addition and subtraction problems. Show how you solved each one.

   A. 156 + 54 = _____   **B.** 232 − 29 = _____

2. Sharon works at a flower shop. She received a shipment of roses and carnations. She received 48 roses. She received 60 more carnations than roses. Show how you solved the following problems.

   A. How many carnations did she receive? _____

   B. How many flowers did she receive in all? _____

100 DAB • Grade 3 • Unit 6   MORE ADDING AND SUBTRACTING

Name _____ Date _____

PART 3

I. Mario covered a piece of paper with base-ten pieces. He used 4 flats and 16 skinnies. Beth said, "That's the same as 416 bits." Is Beth correct? Why or why not? Use base-ten shorthand to show your answer.

2. The middle school collected 1321 canned goods for a charity. The junior high school collected 1299 cans. The high school collected 2219 canned goods.

   A. Which school collected the most canned goods? _____

   B. Which school collected the least? _____

   C. List the numbers from largest to smallest. _____

   D. How many cans were collected in all? _____

PART 4

I. **A.** Ann Marie has some quarters, nickels, and dimes. She has ten coins in all. Half of them are quarters. What is the most money Ann Marie could have? _____ Show how you solved this problem.

   B. What is the least amount Ann Marie could have? _____ Show how you solved this problem.

2. At the zoo, Joe's dad bought 5 snow cones, one for each family member. One snow cone costs $1.26. How much do 5 snow cones cost? _____ Show how you found your answer.

MORE ADDING AND SUBTRACTING   DAB • Grade 3 • Unit 6 101

Glossary

This glossary provides definitions of key vocabulary terms in the Grade 3 lessons. Locations of key vocabulary terms in the curriculum are included with each definition. Components Key: URG = *Unit Resource Guide,* SG = *Student Guide,* and DAB = *Discovery Assignment Book.*

A

Area (URG Unit 5; SG Unit 5)
The area of a shape is the amount of space it covers, measured in square units.

Array (URG Unit 7 & Unit 11)
An array is an arrangement of elements into a rectangular pattern of (horizontal) rows and (vertical) columns. (*See* column and row.)

Associative Property of Addition (URG Unit 2)
For any three numbers a, b, and c we have $a + (b + c) = (a + b) + c$. For example in finding the sum of 4, 8, and 2, one can compute $4 + 8$ first and then add 2: $(4 + 8) + 2 = 14$. Alternatively, we can compute $8 + 2$ and then add the result to 4: $4 + (8 + 2) = 4 + 10 = 14$.

Average (URG Unit 5)
A number that can be used to represent a typical value in a set of data. (*See also* mean and median.)

Axes (URG Unit 8; SG Unit 8)
Reference lines on a graph. In the Cartesian coordinate system, the axes are two perpendicular lines that meet at the origin. The singular of axes is axis.

B

Base (of a cube model) (URG Unit 18; SG Unit 18)
The part of a cube model that sits on the "ground."

Base-Ten Board (URG Unit 4)
A tool to help children organize base-ten pieces when they are representing numbers.

Base-Ten Pieces (URG Unit 4; SG Unit 4)
A set of manipulatives used to model our number system as shown in the figure at the right. Note that a skinny is made of 10 bits, a flat is made of 100 bits, and a pack is made of 1000 bits.

Base-Ten Shorthand (SG Unit 4)
A pictorial representation of the base-ten pieces as shown.

Nickname	Picture	Shorthand
bit	⬜	·
skinny	▭	/
flat	▱	⬜
pack	⬛	⬜

Best-Fit Line (URG Unit 9; SG Unit 9; DAB Unit 9)
The line that comes closest to the most number of points on a point graph.

Bit (URG Unit 4; SG Unit 4)
A cube that measures 1 cm on each edge. It is the smallest of the base-ten pieces that is often used to represent 1. (*See also* base-ten pieces.)

C

Capacity (URG Unit 16)
1. The volume of the inside of a container.
2. The largest volume a container can hold.

Cartesian Coordinate System (URG Unit 8)
A method of locating points on a flat surface by means of numbers. This method is named after its originator, René Descartes. (*See also* coordinates.)

Centimeter (cm)
A unit of measure in the metric system equal to one-hundredth of a meter. (1 inch = 2.54 cm)

Column (URG Unit 11)
In an array, the objects lined up vertically.

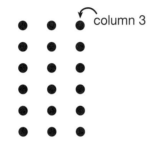
column 3

Common Fraction (URG Unit 15)
Any fraction that is written with a numerator and denominator that are whole numbers. For example, $\frac{3}{4}$ and $\frac{9}{4}$ are both common fractions. (*See also* decimal fraction.)

Commutative Property of Addition (URG Unit 2 & Unit 11)
This is also known as the Order Property of Addition. Changing the order of the addends does not change the sum. For example, $3 + 5 = 5 + 3 = 8$. Using variables, $n + m = m + n$.

Commutative Property of Multiplication (URG Unit 11)
Changing the order of the factors in a multiplication problem does not change the result, e.g., $7 \times 3 = 3 \times 7 = 21$. (*See also* turn-around facts.)

Congruent (URG Unit 12 & Unit 17; SG Unit 12)
Figures with the same shape and size.

Convenient Number (URG Unit 6)
A number used in computation that is close enough to give a good estimate, but is also easy to compute mentally, e.g., 25 and 30 are convenient numbers for 27.

Coordinates (URG Unit 8; SG Unit 8)
An ordered pair of numbers that locates points on a flat surface by giving distances from a pair of coordinate axes. For example, if a point has coordinates (4, 5) it is 4 units from the vertical axis and 5 units from the horizontal axis.

Counting Back (URG Unit 2)
A strategy for subtracting in which students start from a larger number and then count down until the number is reached. For example, to solve $8 - 3$, begin with 8 and count down three, 7, 6, 5.

Counting Down (*See* counting back.)

Counting Up (URG Unit 2)
A strategy for subtraction in which the student starts at the lower number and counts on to the higher number. For example, to solve $8 - 5$, the student starts at 5 and counts up three numbers (6, 7, 8). So $8 - 5 = 3$.

Cube (SG Unit 18)
A three-dimensional shape with six congruent square faces.

Cubic Centimeter (cc)
(URG Unit 16; SG Unit 16)
The volume of a cube that is one centimeter long on each edge.

cubic centimeter

Cup (URG Unit 16)
A unit of volume equal to 8 fluid ounces, one-half pint.

D

Decimal Fraction (URG Unit 15)
A fraction written as a decimal. For example, 0.75 and 0.4 are decimal fractions and $\frac{75}{100}$ and $\frac{4}{10}$ are called common fractions. (*See also* fraction.)

Denominator (URG Unit 13)
The number below the line in a fraction. The denominator indicates the number of equal parts in which the unit whole is divided. For example, the 5 is the denominator in the fraction $\frac{2}{5}$. In this case the unit whole is divided into five equal parts.

Density (URG Unit 16)
The ratio of an object's mass to its volume.

Difference (URG Unit 2)
The answer to a subtraction problem.

Dissection (URG Unit 12 & Unit 17)
Cutting or decomposing a geometric shape into smaller shapes that cover it exactly.

Distributive Property of Multiplication over Addition (URG Unit 19)
For any three numbers *a, b,* and *c, a* $\times$ (*b* + *c*) = *a* $\times$ *b* + *a* $\times$ *c*. The distributive property is the foundation for most methods of multidigit multiplication. For example, $9 \times (17) = 9 \times (10 + 7) = 9 \times 10 + 9 \times 7 = 90 + 63 = 153$.

E

Equal-Arm Balance
See two-pan balance.

Equilateral Triangle (URG Unit 7)
A triangle with all sides of equal length and all angles of equal measure.

Equivalent Fractions (SG Unit 17)
Fractions that have the same value, e.g., $\frac{2}{4} = \frac{1}{2}$.

Estimate (URG Unit 5 & Unit 6)
1. (verb) To find *about* how many.
2. (noun) An approximate number.

Extrapolation (URG Unit 7)
Using patterns in data to make predictions or to estimate values that lie beyond the range of values in the set of data.

F

Fact Family (URG Unit 11; SG Unit 11)
Related math facts, e.g., $3 \times 4 = 12$, $4 \times 3 = 12$, $12 \div 3 = 4$, $12 \div 4 = 3$.

Factor (URG Unit 11; SG Unit 11)
1. In a multiplication problem, the numbers that are multiplied together. In the problem $3 \times 4 = 12$, 3 and 4 are the factors.
2. Whole numbers that can be multiplied together to get a number. That is, numbers that divide a number evenly, e.g., 1, 2, 3, 4, 6, and 12 are all the factors of 12.

Fewest Pieces Rule (URG Unit 4 & Unit 6; SG Unit 4)
Using the least number of base-ten pieces to represent a number. (*See also* base-ten pieces.)

Flat (URG Unit 4; SG Unit 4)
A block that measures 1 cm $\times$ 10 cm $\times$ 10 cm. It is one of the base-ten pieces that is often used to represent 100. (*See also* base-ten pieces.)

Flip (URG Unit 12)
A motion of the plane in which a figure is reflected over a line so that any point and its image are the same distance from the line.

Fraction (URG Unit 15)
A number that can be written as $\frac{a}{b}$ where a and b are whole numbers and b is not zero. For example, $\frac{1}{2}$, 0.5, and 2 are all fractions since 0.5 can be written as $\frac{5}{10}$ and 2 can be written as $\frac{2}{1}$.

Front-End Estimation (URG Unit 6)
Estimation by looking at the left-most digit.

G

Gallon (gal) (URG Unit 16)
A unit of volume equal to four quarts.

Gram
The basic unit used to measure mass.

H

Hexagon (SG Unit 12)
A six-sided polygon.

Horizontal Axis (SG Unit 1)
In a coordinate grid, the x-axis. The axis that extends from left to right.

I

Interpolation (URG Unit 7)
Making predictions or estimating values that lie between data points in a set of data.

J

K

Kilogram
1000 grams.

L

Likely Event (SG Unit 1)
An event that has a high probability of occurring.

Line of Symmetry (URG Unit 12)
A line is a line of symmetry for a plane figure if, when the figure is folded along this line, the two parts match exactly.

Line Symmetry (URG Unit 12; SG Unit 12)
A figure has line symmetry if it has at least one line of symmetry.

Liter (l) (URG Unit 16; SG Unit 16)
Metric unit used to measure volume. A liter is a little more than a quart.

M

Magic Square (URG Unit 2)
A square array of digits in which the sums of the rows, columns, and main diagonals are the same.

Making a Ten (URG Unit 2)
Strategies for addition and subtraction that make use of knowing the sums to ten. For example, knowing $6 + 4 = 10$ can be helpful in finding $10 - 6 = 4$ and $11 - 6 = 5$.

Mass (URG Unit 9 & Unit 16; SG Unit 9)
The amount of matter in an object.

Mean (URG Unit 5)
An average of a set of numbers that is found by adding the values of the data and dividing by the number of values.

Measurement Division (URG Unit 7)
Division as equal grouping. The total number of objects and the number of objects in each group are known. The number of groups is the unknown. For example, tulip bulbs come in packages of 8. If 216 bulbs are sold, how many packages are sold?

Measurement Error (URG Unit 9)
The unavoidable error that occurs due to the limitations inherent to any measurement instrument.

Median (URG Unit 5; DAB Unit 5)
For a set with an odd number of data arranged in order, it is the middle number. For an even number of data arranged in order, it is the number halfway between the two middle numbers.

Meniscus (URG Unit 16; SG Unit 16)
The curved surface formed when a liquid creeps up the side of a container (for example, a graduated cylinder).

Meter (m)
The standard unit of length measure in the metric system. One meter is approximately 39 inches.

Milliliter (ml) (URG Unit 16; SG Unit 16)
A measure of capacity in the metric system that is the volume of a cube that is one centimeter long on each edge.

Multiple (URG Unit 3 & Unit 11)
A number is a multiple of another number if it is evenly divisible by that number. For example, 12 is a multiple of 2 since 2 divides 12 evenly.

N

Numerator (URG Unit 13)
The number written above the line in a fraction. For example, the 2 is the numerator in the fraction $\frac{2}{5}$. (*See also* denominator.)

O

One-Dimensional Object (URG Unit 18; SG Unit 18)
An object is one-dimensional if it is made up of pieces of lines and curves.

Ordered Pairs (URG Unit 8)
A pair of numbers that gives the coordinates of a point on a grid in relation to the origin. The horizontal coordinate is given first; the vertical coordinate is given second. For example, the ordered pair (5, 3) tells us to move five units to the right of the origin and 3 units up.

Origin (URG Unit 8)
The point at which the *x*- and *y*-axes (horizontal and vertical axes) intersect on a coordinate plane. The origin is described by the ordered pair (0, 0) and serves as a reference point so that all the points on the plane can be located by ordered pairs.

P

Pack (URG Unit 4; SG Unit 4)
A cube that measures 10 cm on each edge. It is one of the base-ten pieces that is often used to represent 1000. (*See also* base-ten pieces.)

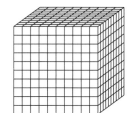

Palindrome (URG Unit 6)
A number, word, or phrase that reads the same forward and backward, e.g., 12321.

Parallel Lines (URG Unit 18)
Lines that are in the same direction. In the plane, parallel lines are lines that do not intersect.

Parallelogram (URG Unit 18)
A quadrilateral with two pairs of parallel sides.

Partitive Division (URG Unit 7)
Division as equal sharing. The total number of objects and the number of groups are known. The number of objects in each group is the unknown. For example, Frank has 144 marbles that he divides equally into 6 groups. How many marbles are in each group?

Pentagon (SG Unit 12)
A five-sided, five-angled polygon.

Perimeter (URG Unit 7; DAB Unit 7)
The distance around a two-dimensional shape.

Pint (URG Unit 16)
A unit of volume measure equal to 16 fluid ounces, i.e., two cups.

Polygon
A two-dimensional connected figure made of line segments in which each endpoint of every side meets with an endpoint of exactly one other side.

Population (URG Unit 1; SG Unit 1)
A collection of persons or things whose properties will be analyzed in a survey or experiment.

Prediction (SG Unit 1)
Using data to declare or foretell what is likely to occur.

Prime Number (URG Unit 11)
A number that has exactly two factors. For example, 7 has exactly two distinct factors, 1 and 7.

Prism
A three-dimensional figure that has two congruent faces, called bases, that are parallel to each other, and all other faces are parallelograms.

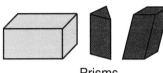

Prisms   Not a prism

Product (URG Unit 11; SG Unit 11; DAB Unit 11)
The answer to a multiplication problem. In the problem $3 \times 4 = 12$, 12 is the product.

Q

Quadrilateral (URG Unit 18)
A polygon with four sides.

Quart (URG Unit 16)
A unit of volume equal to 32 fluid ounces; one quarter of a gallon.

R

Recording Sheet (URG Unit 4)
A place value chart used for addition and subtraction problems.

Rectangular Prism (URG Unit 18; SG Unit 18)
A prism whose bases are rectangles. A right rectangular prism is a prism having all faces rectangles.

Regular (URG Unit 7; DAB Unit 7)
A polygon is regular if all sides are of equal length and all angles are equal.

Remainder (URG Unit 7)
Something that remains or is left after a division problem. The portion of the dividend that is not evenly divisible by the divisor, e.g., $16 \div 5 = 3$ with 1 as a remainder.

Right Angle (SG Unit 12)
An angle that measures 90˚.

Rotation (turn) (URG Unit 12)
A transformation (motion) in which a figure is turned a specified angle and direction around a point.

Row (URG Unit 11)
In an array, the objects lined up horizontally.

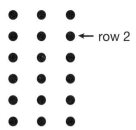

Rubric (URG Unit 2)
A written guideline for assigning scores to student work, for the purpose of assessment.

S

Sample (URG Unit 1; SG Unit 1)
A part or subset of a population.

Skinny (URG Unit 4; SG Unit 4)
A block that measures 1 cm $\times$ 1 cm $\times$ 10 cm. It is one of the base-ten pieces that is often used to represent 10. (*See also* base-ten pieces.)

Square Centimeter (sq cm) (SG Unit 5)
The area of a square that is 1 cm long on each side.

Square Number (SG Unit 11)
A number that is the product of a whole number multiplied by itself. For example, 25 is a square number since $5 \times 5 = 25$. A square number can be represented by a square array with the same number of rows as columns. A square array for 25 has 5 rows of 5 objects in each row or 25 total objects.

Standard Masses
A set of objects with convenient masses, usually 1 g, 10 g, 100 g, etc.

Sum (URG Unit 2; SG Unit 2)
The answer to an addition problem.

Survey (URG Unit 14; SG Unit 14)
An investigation conducted by collecting data from a sample of a population and then analyzing it. Usually surveys are used to make predictions about the entire population.

T

Tangrams (SG Unit 12)
A type of geometric puzzle. A shape is given and it must be covered exactly with seven standard shapes called tans.

Thinking Addition (URG Unit 2)
A strategy for subtraction that uses a related addition problem. For example, $15 - 7 = 8$ because $8 + 7 = 15$.

Three-Dimensional (URG Unit 18; SG Unit 18)
Existing in three-dimensional space; having length, width, and depth.

TIMS Laboratory Method (URG Unit 1; SG Unit 1)
A method that students use to organize experiments and investigations. It involves four components: draw, collect, graph, and explore. It is a way to help students learn about the scientific method.

Turn (URG Unit 12)
(*See* rotation.)

Turn-Around Facts (URG Unit 2 & Unit 11 p. 37; SG Unit 11)
Addition facts that have the same addends but in a different order, e.g., $3 + 4 = 7$ and $4 + 3 = 7$. (*See also* commutative property of addition and commutative property of multiplication.)

Two-Dimensional (URG Unit 18; SG Unit 18)
Existing in the plane; having length and width.

Two-Pan Balance
A device for measuring the mass of an object by balancing the object against a number of standard masses (usually multiples of 1 unit, 10 units, and 100 units, etc.).

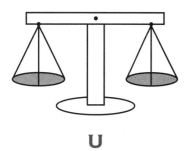

U

Unit (of measurement) (URG Unit 18)
A precisely fixed quantity used to measure. For example, centimeter, foot, kilogram, and quart are units of measurement.

Using a Ten (URG Unit 2)
1. A strategy for addition that uses partitions of the number 10. For example, one can find $8 + 6$ by thinking $8 + 6 = 8 + 2 + 4 = 10 + 4 = 14$.
2. A strategy for subtraction that uses facts that involve subtracting 10. For example, students can use $17 - 10 = 7$ to learn the "close fact" $17 - 9 = 8$.

Using Doubles (URG Unit 2)
Strategies for addition and subtraction that use knowing doubles. For example, one can find $7 + 8$ by thinking $7 + 8 = 7 + 7 + 1 = 14 + 1 = 15$. Knowing $7 + 7 = 14$ can be helpful in finding $14 - 7 = 7$ and $14 - 8 = 6$.

V

Value (URG Unit 1; SG Unit 1)
The possible outcomes of a variable. For example, red, green, and blue are possible values for the variable *color*. Two meters and 1.65 meters are possible values for the variable *length*.

Variable (URG Unit 1; SG Unit 1)
1. An attribute or quantity that changes or varies.
2. A symbol that can stand for a variable.

Vertex (URG Unit 12; SG Unit 12)
1. A point where the sides of a polygon meet.
2. A point where the edges of a three-dimensional object meet.

Vertical Axis (SG Unit 1)
In a coordinate grid, the y-axis. It is perpendicular to the horizontal axis.

Volume (URG Unit 16; SG Unit 16)
The measure of the amount of space occupied by an object.

Volume by Displacement (URG Unit 16)
A way of measuring volume of an object by measuring the amount of water (or some other fluid) it displaces.

W

Weight (URG Unit 9)
A measure of the pull of gravity on an object. One unit for measuring weight is the pound.

X

Y

Z